WHILE I REMEMBER

by

ANTHONY BUCKERIDGE

With an introduction by David Bathurst

DS
David Schutte

First published in 1999 by Romansmead Publications

This slightly revised edition published in 1999 by

David Schutte
119 Sussex Road
Petersfield
Hampshire GU31 4LB

3 5 7 9 8 6 4 2

Radio Times cover reproduced by kind permission

Printed in the U.K. by Polestar AUP Aberdeen Ltd

ISBN 0 9521482 1 8

British Library Cataloguing-in-Publication Data.
A catalogue record for this book is available from the British Library.

EILEEN - her book

Radio Times (Incorporating World-Radio)
September, 24, 1954. Vol. 124: No. 1611
Registered at the G.P.O. as a Newspaper

SOUND AND TELEVISIO
SEPTEMBER 26—OCTOBER

RADIO TIMES

JOURNAL OF THE BBC PRICE THREEPENCE

Jennings joins the Light Programme

Anthony Buckeridge, author of the schoolboy plays which have long been so popular in Children's Hour, is seen with Jennings (Glyn Dearman) on the left and Darbishire (Henry Searle)

'PRINCESS IDA'
Act 2 of the Gilbert and Sullivan opera from the Savoy Theatre (Monday)

SIR ADRIAN BOULT
Four broadcasts with the BBC Symphony Orchestra

EARTHQUAKE IN ALGERIA
A BBC team reports on a visit to the scene of the disaster (Sunday)

BOB MONKHOUSE
in 'Fast and Loose' (Wednesday TV)

CLAUDIO ARRAU
A television recital on Wednesday

TOP OF THE FORM
returns to the Light Programme (Monday)

VIC OLIVER
returns to 'Variety Playhouse' (Saturday)

VERA LYNN, MAX MILLER
in television Music-Hall (Saturday)

DICK BENTLEY
opens his new television show (Friday)

INTRODUCTION

by

David Bathurst

Anthony Buckeridge is the author of a series of plays and books which made him famous. In these works we are introduced to Jennings, a fictional schoolboy at Linbury Court Preparatory School, Linbury, near Dunhambury in Sussex.

I became a devotee of the Jennings stories before I was ten years old. My first Jennings book was given to me by my grandfather on Christmas Day 1966, but slowly I began to build up the collection until a few years later I acquired the complete set. I have particularly fond memories of my acquisition of my second title at the age of seven. It was a Saturday afternoon in February 1967 and we were in the pleasant Hampshire town of Alresford. As we were about to set off for home a few miles away, my father ushered me into Lawrence's Bookshop (sadly long since defunct) and invited me to choose another Jennings book. That was over thirty years ago, but adulthood, far from diminishing my love of the titles, has increased it.

During the 1980s I made a number of moves in the course of my legal studies, and when I finally settled in the Chichester area, I found to my consternation that many books in my Jennings collection had disappeared. I must confess that they would not have been worth much to a collector, as most of the dustjackets had not survived. Nonetheless, after various enquiries proved fruitless, I decided to build up the collection again, not as an investment, but out of a love for the delightful characters and brilliant prose that made the books such a joy to read. As I rebuilt the collection – fortunately, the process was not difficult – I decided to translate my enthusiasm for the stories into something tangible. Hence in 1994 I commenced work on *The Jennings Companion*. This appeared in late 1995. The aim of the Companion was to provide the existing or potential Jennings enthusiast with all the information about the set of twenty-five Jennings books. It provided a synopsis of each book, with details of publication dates, illustrators, and values of first editions. It also gave light-hearted analyses of each principal character, and an A-Z of the themes and minor characters in the books. Moreover, it provided details of all the radio plays and listed other publications and programmes in which Jennings stories had appeared.

The Companion was a great success and remains the only definitive book "about" the Jennings stories.

This of course does not give me any sort of monopoly on books about Jennings and his creator. Nonetheless, my almost lifelong enthusiasm for the books, combined with the extensive reading I had to undertake to produce the Companion, gives me arguably as broad a knowledge of the stories as anybody else. I am also very fortunate in that living, as I do, within easy reach of Anthony and his lovely wife Eileen, it has been easy for me to maintain face-to-face as well as telephone contact with them. Both supported me very loyally as I assembled the Companion, and it was I who was approached to write an introduction to Anthony's autobiography.

I have decided to use the opportunity presented by the completion of Anthony's life-story to bring the Companion, in a sense, up to date with an extended introduction. However, that is all it is; an introduction or aperitif before the main meal, the story of Anthony's first eighty-six years.

Appearances can be deceptive. A visitor to Anthony's beautiful house might go up to his study with its fine views to the South Downs, and reflect on what a gentle and uncomplicated life he must lead, writing books about schoolboys. Perusal of his autobiography tells a different story; a story that begins tragically with the loss of his father in horrific circumstances, and far from portraying a life of ivory-towered sanctuary demonstrates how hard Anthony did have to work to achieve his status and fame. Readers anxious to hear how the Jennings books originated will not be disappointed; but the book contains many other nuggets which will be of great interest not only from what they tell us about Anthony, but about twentieth-century living. I commend it to you and trust you will enjoy reading about Anthony's real life as much as we have enjoyed the lives of the fictional characters that he created.

All that will come later in the book. For now, however, I want to consider Jennings since the Companion.

The rest of this section is divided into two parts. In the first part, I reproduce a number of excellent articles in praise of Jennings, which have been made available to me since the Companion appeared. In the second part, I take the story of Jennings a stage further. The profile of Jennings and his creator has been raised significantly by some recent events, and since this book is being prepared on the verge of the new Millennium, it seems eminently appropriate to look back on these events and also speculate on what the future holds for Jennings and his friends beyond 2000.

Following publication of the Companion, I received a number of witty and apposite articles about fellow Jennings lovers. I would certainly have wished to include them in the Companion had they been available at the time. The first, *Schoolmasterpiece* by Mike Seabrook, compares Jennings with another mischievous fictional schoolboy, William Brown. The second, *Especially Jennings* by Terence Paul Smith, is a more general appraisal.

SCHOOLMASTERPIECE

by Mike Seabrook

I suspect that if a representative sample of people of my generation (I was born in 1950) were asked which were the favourite books of their childhood, it would be a close thing between Richmal Crompton's William Brown stories, and Arthur Ransome's tales of the Swallows and the Amazons.

Both these series were and remain truly great literature, reaching far beyond the prisoning boundaries of the pigeon-hole "children's literature." In the end, though, despite their formidable claims to be the greatest books originally written for children this century, I go for another series of novels about children; the Jennings books of Anthony Buckeridge. And, unlike the Ransome and Crompton sequences, this series throws up a single, clear candidate to be considered the best of the lot.

Comparisons are odious, but a few have to be drawn to show why I choose these stories over their more celebrated rivals. First, although Buckeridge's children are as unmistakably middle-class as Ransome's, they are far more human. If Ransome's children have a fault, it is that they are more than a bit too good to be true, to the point where one really wishes one could, just once, catch them in some kind of rebellion or delinquency. But no; they never once, in 12 chunky volumes, so much as hint at the slightest redeeming vice. Buckeridge's kids, on the other hand, are regularly naughty; never violent, never delinquent, just occasionally prone to lapses of manners, judgment, obedience and behaviour – they are, in fact, *normal.*

Even the Hubert Lane gang wouldn't accuse William and Co. of being good; but they falter in comparison with Buckeridge's characters mainly because they come from an earlier age. So, while William himself is ageless and timeless, the eternal naughty boy clamouring to escape the trammels of conformity in all of us, the stories are dated, remote from us in too many superficial aspects. Buckeridge's stories treat of here and now.

One of the biggest single factors in my choice of these preparatory school tales is that while all the children in all three series are utterly believable (the quibble about Ransome's being too good to be true is easily forgettable amid the fast-moving excellence of the plots), the adults in both the Ransome and Crompton are often somewhat two-dimensional, little more than stage props for the really important characters. In Buckeridge, the lethally accurate portrayals of the boys are more than merely supported by the characters of three schoolmasters, Mr Carter, the headmaster and, especially and unforgettably, Mr Wilkins.

Perhaps the greatest accolade I can bestow on these stories is that they are among the very, very few books ever to have made me literally cry with laughter – which they did when I first met Jennings and Co when I was nine and still do to this day – and as often as not, it is not the antics of the boys that have me in convulsions, but those of L.P. Wilkins, Esq., MA (Cantab).

There are other things, too; the boys' attempts to decipher the spidery handwriting of Jennings' Aunt Angela had me in hysterics; so did the episode of the delivery van and the bicycle, the unannounced visit of a Schools Inspector and many others. But more often than not, if you find me doubled up, howling like a wolf and clutching ribs that really do hurt, *cherchez* Mr Wilkins. Reading the episode of Wilkins, the alarm clock and Tennyson's *In Memoriam* is one of the most painful, and joyous, experiences of my life.

Apart from his propensity to get into the most magnificent but wholly believable muddles, it is through Wilkins's mouth that Buckeridge produces some of the most splendid plays on words; "It's…it's uncannibal," he splutters on one occasion; on another he produces the wonderful apparition of "the insanitary spectre," conjuring up visions of an unhygienic ghost.

But for me Wilkins's finest hour is without doubt his performance as Police Sergeant Snodgrass in my choice as the very best of a magnificent series, *Jennings Follows a Clue.* This is one of the earliest Jennings stories, first published in 1953; but the humour is as fresh and undated as humour itself.

It is also one of the remarkably few seamlessly credible boy-detective stories, and includes what is quite possibly the finest travelling salesman story ever written. The portrait of the headmaster, who is precisely what one would expect someone called Martin Winthrop Barlow Pemberton-Oakes, MA (Oxon) to be, is a small masterpiece in itself – a schoolmasterpiece, one might say, and that would be a good word to describe this wonderful book all round.

ESPECIALLY JENNINGS!

by Terence Paul Smith

When I was asked, along with other colleagues, to name my five favourite children's books for *Book Week*, I had no hesitation in placing Anthony Buckeridge's *A Bookful of Jennings* at the head of my list – although any of the individual Jennings books would have served instead.

I was first introduced to Jennings and his friends when I was about eleven years old and was given a copy of *Jennings' Little Hut* as a Sunday school prize. I read it eagerly, and thereafter acquired other books in the series, including the first in the sequence, *Jennings Goes to School*. For a while too I followed the exploits of this favourite schoolboy hero in *The Children's Newspaper*, a weekly publication now defunct. Throughout the 1950s and 60s Jennings and his pal Darbishire were extremely popular. They appeared not only in book form and in *The Children's Newspaper*, but also in other publications, such as the BBC's *The Children's Hour Annual* (e.g. for 1951). *Jennings At School* became a much-listened-to series on BBC Radio's *Children's Hour*, whilst *Jennings Abounding* was a successful BBC TV children's television series. There have been records and audio tapes; and a number of films in Norway.

For despite being set in an oh-so-English boys' preparatory school (somewhere near the Sussex coast and a few miles from the imaginary town of Dunhambury), the Jennings series was translated into at least twelve languages, including Danish, Dutch, Finnish, French, German, Hebrew, Norwegian, Spanish, Swedish and Welsh, even though in most of the countries where these languages are spoken "boarding schools are unknown and school uniform unheard of!" (publisher's note on the jacket of *A Bookful of Jennings*). The very name "Jennings" is English and has often been changed for consumption abroad.

As an apprehensive and understandably homesick new boy at Linbury

Court School in *Jennings Goes to School*, John Christopher Timothy Jennings is an engaging ten-year-old, and of the same age is his best friend, Charles Edwin Jeremy Darbishire, son of a clergyman. But later both boys attain their eleventh birthdays, and eleven they remain throughout the rest of the series. It was a judicious choice. There would be a large measure of agreement that eleven tends to be one of the most contented and carefree years in a child's life. Which is not to say, of course, that there are not individual problems and concerns. There are, and Jennings certainly has his share of them – always dragging poor Darbishire into them too. But of course it is always possible to blame others: "After all, that hoo-hah the other night was all Sir's fault, really. If only he'd listened to your advice... everything would have been all right," Darbishire consoles his friend after a flooded bath has brought down the ceiling of the room beneath in *The Trouble with Jennings*. Trouble springs largely from Jennings' liveliness, from his willingness to help, from his remarkable ability to misunderstand and muddle, and from ineffective attempts to put right what has already gone wrong.

Jennings is described as "a touselled-headed boy... with a friendly expression on his face and a wide-awake look in his eyes" (*Just Like Jennings)*. Similar statements are found in most of the books. He "had about him the eager air of one who acts first and thinks afterwards. Though full of good intentions, his well-sprung plans were apt to recoil and his shafts of inspiration to fall wide of their target" (*Jennings of Course*). The long-suffering Darbishire is very different: "Fair-haired and curly, with mild blue eyes beneath his ink-spotted glasses, he is a staunch follower but never a leader..." (*A Bookful of Jennings*). Only very occasionally do the two boys quarrel, and then things are soon patched up.

Other boys also appear in the stories, most of them class-mates in Form III; the untidy Venables, usually trailing unfastened shoe-laces, Temple, Atkinson ("Atki"), Bromwich ("Bromo"), Martin-Jones, and Rumbelow; then there are the younger boys: Bromwich II, Binns, and Blotwell (a splendid name for a schoolboy!) All are under the charge of the stern but basically kindly Headmaster, Mr Pemberton-Oakes ("The Arch-beak") and his senior master, Mr Carter, who has a good understanding of the schoolboy mind. Not so the irascible Mr Wilkins, whose adult mind can never really understand the often illogical ways in which schoolboys choose to act. But he too, beneath it all, has a great affection for the misunderstood boys for whom he is responsible. There must be many schoolteachers who are able to sympathise with his position! Mr Hind is the rather more dreamy music master, and Matron is always ready to lend a sympathetic ear and to sort out troubles, medical and otherwise – including acute cases of twisted-belt-buckle-itis ("Wow! That sounds bad," Jennings exclaimed. "Shall I have to see the doctor, Matron?" "Oh, no, it's not serious." She straightened out the twisted belt and slackened the adjustable buckle at the back, which had ridden up over the waistband of his shorts. "There, that's done it...." *According to Jennings*). Other adults make their appearances from time to time – including the delightful Jack Carr and his car-jack (*Thanks to Jennings*).

In *Written for Children* (2nd edition, 1974), John Rowe Townsend is rather dismissive: "Anthony Buckeridge's Jennings series....(was) extremely popular, if of no great literary merit." But in the journal *Growing Point* Margery Fisher is much warmer, commending the books' "inventive skill and unobtrusive good style." Nicholas Tucker, writing both as literary critic and child psychologist, in *The Child and the Book* (1981), refers to the appeal of Jennings in allowing young readers "to work off aggression against adults in the imagination, but without ever having to face up to what they are doing, since... most of the disasters that Jennings causes happen because he is trying to help; a kind of unconscious aggression, perhaps, but one that children still seem to find entertaining in print." There is a good deal of truth in this position, and certainly there is far less overt aggression than in, say, the William series of books, where William's relationship to his father seems decidedly Oedipal. On the other hand, some of Jennings' relationships with adults are warm and friendly with no hint of even a disguised or covert aggression. Most enthusiastic of all in support of Jennings is Joseph Connolly in *Children's Modern First Editions* (1988): "the funniest and best-written schoolboy books, bar none. Buckeridge is now enjoying a richly-deserved revival following a dip in popularity during the seventies and eighties." Amen to that!

The books are undeniably middle-class in their ethos – they are, after all, set in a boys' fee-paying preparatory (and mainly boarding) school, though without the hint of snobbery which sometimes crept into Frank Richards' Billy Bunter, Tom Merry, and other school stories and which so shocked George Orwell when he was pretending to be working-class (actually he was educated at Eton!). Certainly Jennings is more firmly rooted in his class background than, say, Richmal Crompton's William Brown, who in his manner of speaking, for example, slips out of his stockbroker-belt background in order to become the engaging (or not, according to taste!) urchin.

It is precisely this consistency, and Jennings' essential boyishness, which enable the books to speak immediately to children of any background. All the more reason, therefore, to share Joseph Connolly's misgivings about the revisions of the latest reprints – revised by Buckeridge himself – published by Goodchild in hardback and by Macmillan in paperback. (The original books were published by Collins in hardback, except for the last Collins title, *Jennings at Large*, 1977, which was an original Armada paperback; there were subsequent hardback and paperback editions, including two in Puffin Books – *Jennings Goes to School* and *Our Friend Jennings*; some were also issued by Collins in small-format school editions.) Some of the changes were perhaps advisable; the word "gay," having somewhat changed its meaning, has been replaced, and references to staff smoking have been cut out. (Joseph Connolly's comment on this, echoing Mr Wilkins, is "I – I – Corwumph!") On the jackets of the hardbacks, and as explained in a newspaper interview in 1985, short trousers and school caps have been omitted, despite the fact that the latter play important roles in some of the stories, notably in *Our Friend Jennings*, where much trouble is caused when Jennings loses his cap on an illicit visit to the cinema. And, of course, both items are still part of compulsory uniform for many preparatory schools. Sensibly, Macmillan's illustrator Rodney Sutton has restored the short trousers and caps – sensibly, because part of the appeal of these books must be their evocation of a different world from that of most of their readers. This is not just a matter of passing time – it always was so. Young readers like myself, who, unlike George Orwell, really did come from a working-class background, were always outside the Jennings world – and it didn't matter in the least. I never experienced prep., still less boarding school life; I never called my headmaster the "Archbeak," or teachers "beaks;" I never described people who let me down as "izzard oiks;" and my exclamations have always been somewhat more basic than "Fossilised fish-hooks!" When I first came across Jennings' "hic haec hoc" I had not started Latin and had no idea what this strange incantation was all about. (I pronounced the middle word to myself as "hay-ek" – which doubtless will make Latin teachers squirm!) Again, this just did not matter, for Jennings' character was what was important and the unfamiliarity of his school was easily accommodated.

What was good, and appealing about the Jennings books was – and is – that they can transcend any divisions, since Jennings is, at bottom, simply an archetypal eleven-year-old schoolboy. His well-meaning but misguided efforts to help are universal, as is his mixture of respect and disdain for adults – particularly teachers. Teachers, and headmasters especially, are regarded as rather strange specimens, scarcely at home in the real world – not a bad judgment, one would think! Above all, Jennings' mischievous attitude, unsullied by any genuine nastiness or self-seeking, is an enduring quality which ought to appeal to many children and adults today.

The escapades with the cart-wheel in the museum (and at school!); the episode of locking General Merridew in the School Library; the cross-country run accomplished by bus; the hut-building (and collapse!) on the island; Irving Borrowmore's rescue, at the last minute, of the excerpt from Henry V; the scientific frogman; the shattering alarm-clock intended as a present for Mr Wilkins who is not in fact leaving; the Headmaster's vain attempt to use a typewriter ("NOT ICE...In fiyutre no buys will be preMnitted to bluild nuts ub the neiHghbourhoof uf the pond? & the a£5rea will be plAvced ou98t of hounds"); the makeshift space-helmet stuck on Jennings' head; the well-intentioned, and eventually successful, Old Folks At Home; the coming and going of articles at the local Jumble Sale – all these and many, many more are episodes of lasting good-natured humour.

"Why, I bet you a million pounds nobody in their senses would ever want to read stories about boys like us!" said Jennings.

On the other side of the door Mr Carter smiled. "Wouldn't they?" he murmured. "I'm not so sure." (*Jennings Goes To School*)

They did. And they do. Especially Jennings!

*

Peter Cross, a freelance journalist from Kent, wrote the following piece in the summer of 1998 which was submitted to, but not published in, *The Oldie* magazine:

Anthony Buckeridge, author of the Jennings books, is alive and well. While Jennings, the prep schoolboy hero of two dozen books, 62 *Children's Hour* radio plays, two TV series and more recently a musical, remains forever eleven, his creator at 86 makes few concessions to the passage of time. He may have lost the use of an eye, be frailer than he was, and may take things a little easier, but in most respects he is as sharp, as observant and as amused as ever.

For the past 35 years Mr Buckeridge and his wife Eileen have lived in a home they have bought and enlarged just inland from Lewes in a stunning Sussex landscape. Anthony still writes. He works from a first floor study producing longhand prose, which is typed up by Eileen. Work is slow, each page having to be right before he can move to the next.

Mr Buckeridge is unlikely to write another Jennings story. Macmillan already have more than they need. Instead he is working on what he describes as a quiet autobiography; he says he hasn't led the sort of spectacular life needed for a best-seller. Actually, he has more than enough good material; his father was killed in the First World War and he received an education of sorts in a deprived twenties boarding school. Then there is a working life that has included employment as a bank clerk, wartime fireman and actor. He was, like Richmal Crompton (author of the *William* books), a schoolteacher before becoming a full-time writer. Unlike her it was his choice to give up teaching rather than being forced out through ill health.

It is interesting to compare Jennings with William Brown. William, feels Buckeridge, is a rebel, whilst Jennings is anything but. Indeed, Jennings gets into trouble trying to avoid it. He might attempt to get the better of a teacher like Mr Wilkins, but will never be rude. William on the other hand is far more streetwise and has little difficulty getting the better of most adults. He dominates the Outlaws and, indeed, his creator, who complained of being tyrannised by him. Buckeridge, it would seem, is far more comfortable with the gentler, more naïve, Jennings.

The books were updated in the late seventies when Jennings moved publishing houses from Collins to Macmillan. The author was very much against this, feeling that the stories were of their time. But it was pointed out that contemporary children would not know what a tuppeny ice cream was, or a fourpenny bus ride. Words like gay and queer, which had taken on a new meaning, were also changed.

Jennings has been translated into twelve languages including Chinese and Hebrew. He has always been popular in France and especially in Norway (where he is known as Stompa), and continues to thrive.

Children's literature, and the people who produce it, have become one source of avid collecting. Anthony Buckeridge is no exception, having been adopted by the Old Boys Book Club (Northern section) who have made him their Vice President. "I used to throw away my old manuscripts," he says.

"Now I find I can sell them for lots of money."

Recently there was a Jennings Day held in a hotel in Lewes, which included extracts from the Jennings musical, an interview of Buckeridge by Michael Crick (a *Newsnight* reporter and lifelong Jennings fan), and a quiz set by Crick's ten-year-old daughter. The author of the stories felt he did fairly well to have got eight out of ten correct, but was soundly beaten by one of his readers. Michael Crick tells me that last year a novice teacher from Hackney came to a Jennings day and explained that she was struggling with a class of unruly 7-year-olds in a school that had just failed its OFSTED test. She couldn't get them interested in reading or writing, having tried stories from every writer she could think of. She eventually read them a Jennings story, and they were hooked - to the extent that the class were soon reading the books for themselves and writing their own stories. So successful was this that she designed the whole curriculum around Jennings. Maths was Jennings and Darbishire going to the tuckshop with 75p and buying three bars of chocolate for 18p each; geography involved drawing a map of Linbury where the stories are set, and so forth. "What's so amazing," says Crick, "is that kids from inner-city Hackney, many from backgrounds like Kurdistan, should have been interested in stories set in a rural all-boys prep school in the 1950s and 60s."

But should we be surprised that these stories appeal to latter-day children? They are, of course, of their time - but perhaps that is their charm. Jennings, Darbishire and the rest are still recognisable. Jennings' warped logic and the trouble it gets him into is still something that today's young can identify with. There is also something very comforting about this enclosed world where fair play and decency always win the day.

*

The following letter from Ian Farrington to Anthony Buckeridge dated 26th June 1996 is typical of hundreds that Anthony Buckeridge has received over the years:

"Noting with pleasure and amusement your letter in today's Guardian, *I take the opportunity to thank you for all the fun and sheer joy your Jennings books have given myself and others for thirty years or more. Jennings and Darbishire have been part of my mental furniture since I had* Jennings Goes

to School *for a Christmas present in the 1950s. Along with Richmal Crompton's William books, you remain one of the immortals of laughter and good sense. I am delighted to see you are still going (strongly, I trust); best wishes and thanks.*

"I will just add that my own schooldays were nothing like those depicted in the prep-school environment, as I attended a secondary modern school, but clearly the humour is universal. Later, I became a schoolteacher (comprehensives) and eventually a University lecturer, meeting not a few Mr Wilkinses on the way; I hope my own performances have been more Mr Carter-like.

"My own four children are fairly baffled by some of the details in the books, but I hope to convince them of your worth as they mature. For myself, I hope never to be too old to fail to appreciate 'Home Made Cakes And Bicycles Repaired' or Jack Carr's Car Jack.

"My most sincere appreciation to you, Sir."

In 1997 Anthony celebrated his 85th birthday. In honour of this, there was a special BBC broadcast, which Anthony himself describes in his autobiography, which follows. This went out on his birthday, June 20th. Then, on June 21st, the first "Jennings Meeting" was held, in Leicester. The brains behind the meeting was Darrell Swift of the Northern section of the Old Boys Book Club, an organisation which – as its name implies – aims to promote and maintain a healthy interest in bygone children's literature. Jennings enthusiasts from all over the country were invited to attend the meeting. During the morning, the enthusiasts gathered and spent some hours in informal discussion; there was also ample opportunity to exchange Jennings literature and other memorabilia. After lunch the formal part of the meeting began. Darrell Swift gave a brief introduction; Anthony's wife Eileen then spoke briefly, after which Anthony read an extract from *Just Like Jennings*. I myself gave a talk on correspondence in the Jennings stories, which was extremely well received, following which the writer and literary critic Mary Cadogan took a more academic look at the stories and their literary context. Then came the Hackney schoolteacher Jane-Louise Godfrey's very moving presentation, which has been alluded to by Peter Cross in his article above. After tea, and delicious birthday cake, came a quiz from Catherine Crick. An enthusiast from South Shields talked of his passion for the stories, the book dealer David Schutte played one of the Children's Hour tapes, and there was a question session with Anthony.

The day was such a success that, although it was not felt appropriate to establish a Jennings Society as such, it was agreed to hold a similar function in 1998. This took place on 20th June at Lewes, East Sussex, being the town nearest to Anthony's home. The formal part of the meeting began with short contributions from Anthony's son-in-law Ted Herrington, Darrell Swift and Mary Cadogan, then two enthusiasts Peter Hicks and Jonathan Cooper spoke respectively about the illustrators in the Jennings books (a digest of his talk appears as an appendix to this book) and Latin in the Jennings stories. Another quiz from Catherine (alluded to by Peter Cross above) followed, I spoke about the poems in the stories, then after tea Anthony did another question session. The item which was by popular consensus the highlight of the day came next, as Anthony and Eileen's son Corin joined with Anthony in singing extracts from the Jennings musical. A similar event is planned in 1999.

During 1998 further material appeared which would be of some interest to Jennings connoisseurs. In August of that year at least two national newspapers wrote of the "discovery" of Diarmaid Jennings, the "real" Jennings who gave Anthony the inspiration for some of the early plots in the Jennings stories. Anthony discusses this more in his autobiography. Later in 1998 the *Radio Times Guide to TV Comedy* provided all the details of the two Jennings BBC television series. It is believed that no other book in print carries this information. The first series ran from 6th September to 8th November 1958 – ten thirty-minute episodes going out on Saturday evenings, mostly at 5.10pm. Kevin Sheldon was the producer. Jennings was played by John Mitchell, Darbishire by Derek Needs, Atkinson by Jeremy Ward, Temple by Peter Wood, Venables by Colin Spaull, Mr Carter by Geoffrey Wincott and Mr Wilkins by Wilfred Babbage. (Both Wincott and Babbage took part in the radio plays as well.) The second series ran from 5th September to 10th October 1966 – six twenty-five minute episodes going out on Monday evenings at 5.25pm. This time Jennings was played by David Schulten, Darbishire by Robert Bartlett, Atkinson by Edward McMurray, Temple by William Burleigh, Venables by Iain Burton, Mr Carter by Ian Gardiner and Mr Wilkins by John Moore. Johnny Downes was the producer.

I could not resist a smile when I found that Homer Simpson, the nominal head of the famous American cartoon family, had adopted the catchphrase "Doh!" when he wished to express frustration. *The Radio Times Guide to TV Comedy* tells us that according to Dan Castellaneta, who provides

Homer's voice, this was lifted from James Finlayson, whose similar utterance was a regular feature of the *Laurel and Hardy* films. Jennings enthusiasts will of course think of L.P.Wilkins Esq first....

As Jennings approaches the Millennium, there are good and bad signs. It is clear that the Jennings books do not enjoy the high profile in children's literature that they once did, and in many children's sections of bookshops it can be extremely difficult to find a copy even of the newly edited paperback Jennings stories. Many of the guides to children's literature, written for adults to assist them in finding suitable books for their children to read, have seen fit to exclude the Jennings stories altogether.

There are, however, some encouraging portents. There is still a thriving market for Jennings books amongst collectors, and the fact that sufficient numbers have expressed interest in not one, but multiple Jennings meetings, demonstrates that there is still tremendous affection for Jennings and his loyal friend Darbishire. The story of the "discovery" of Diarmaid Jennings was felt to be of sufficient importance to be a lead story on one of the inside pages of *The Times* in August 1998. Anthony still receives many complimentary and congratulatory letters from all over the world. There is no reason to believe that this undercurrent of affection for Jennings, and the pleasure that reading of his exploits has brought, will diminish significantly for many years.

One thing on which Anthony will not be drawn is what might have happened to Jennings as an adult. One or two authors have written plays or short stories which project Jennings and Darbishire into the future; one example of this is John Cargill Thompson's play *Jennings and Darbishire Twenty Years On*, which was first produced with Anthony's permission in Edinburgh in August 1993. In reality, however, Russell Newmark summed it up most eloquently when he wrote in 1991:

"He (Jennings) should be in his early fifties by now, probably married with children, his schooldays just a distant memory. But J.C.T. Jennings stays frozen in time, fated to be the perpetual 11-year-old."

And that, one guesses, is how most people would prefer him to remain.

WHILE I REMEMBER

by

Anthony Buckeridge

1

My father was a poet who worked in a bank; he was killed in action in 1917. The official War Office postcard merely said "Missing, believed killed," but there was really no doubt. What the postcard meant was *demolished without trace*.

It was the night of 3rd May at Bullecourt, near Arras. A depleted company of men were ordered to recapture a fortified village from which a whole battalion of allied soldiers had been forced to withdraw a few days before. The stupidity of the order was unbelievable, the result disastrous.

My father's contingent of the Honourable Artillery Company had arrived at the front for the first time that morning. At eleven o'clock that night they were ordered to achieve the impossible. A few were lucky enough to survive, but by the early hours of the next morning most of them were dead.

So, after months of forming fours and shooting at cardboard targets, Dad was sent to face the enemy with no cover but flooded shell-holes. His war had lasted half an hour and had achieved nothing; after that, annihilation. No grave for there was no body to bury. Not even any pieces.

Hope and uncertainty kept my mother and grandmother seeking for news for months afterwards. A colleague who survived the attack and was the last man to see Dad alive wrote to my mother suggesting that he might have been taken prisoner. He was trying to dilute the despair with a little hope but, as he must surely have known, it was the most fragile of straws to clutch at.

All this meant nothing to me, a four-year-old. I knew that Daddy had gone to war, which explained why he no longer came home in the evening to play with me at bedtime and make up little rhymes to amuse me. I was told that he would come home when the war was over; but he never came. And I accepted this with a child's acceptance of something he could not understand. The reality came later, and came imperceptibly.

It was towards the end of the war when we were back in London that one day I said (I think for the first time) “I want my Daddy.” My mother wept.

It came as a shock to me to realise that something I said could make Mum cry. My feeling of needing my Daddy brought with it an uneasy awareness of vicarious authority. I was both fascinated and alarmed by this new sense of power; I could make my mother cry. Now, eighty years later, I still feel guilty about this; but children are insensitive about other people’s feelings. They learn as they grow up.

To begin with, Mother and I stayed in London after Dad had gone. There were air raids; Mother watched a Zeppelin being brought down in flames but I was too sleepy to wake up, and there was a daylight raid while I was playing outside with our neighbour’s children. We were hustled indoors but, to my chagrin, my wooden horse Dobbin was left out on the path with the enemy aeroplanes in view. I wanted to run out to rescue my Dobbin. I argued that I could make a quick dash, dodging any bombs that happened to be raining down (by jumping sideways, perhaps?). I lost the argument and no bombs fell in the vicinity. Shortly afterwards we went to stay with my grandparents at Ross-on-Wye and then with my Aunt Kate in Cornwall.

Our London home was in Holly Village, Highgate, N6. The village is now an anachronism holding its own and surrounded by expensive flats and houses. It consists of twelve small, dark-gabled and ecclesiastically-windowed dwellings built to house the workers of the Burdett-Coutts estate in the 1850s. It’s charming, it’s unique, it’s out of this world, though John Betjeman didn’t like the look of it much when he wrote in *Summoned by Bells*:

> *“And Holly Village with its prickly roofs*
> *Against the sky were terrifying shapes.”*

But maybe it was too near Highgate Cemetery for him. For Betjeman lived in nearby up-market West Hill. He was a little older than me and I never met him.

Of the twelve families of Holly Village two were the proud owners of a motor-car though none boasted a telephone. The lack of a phone didn't seem to bother anyone very much; the postal service was excellent. You could send a postcard in the morning inviting someone to tea on the same day and the guest would have received the invitation by lunch time. There was no electricity, but we had gas – downstairs at any rate for the smaller bedrooms were candle-lit. The houses stood like semi-detached islands in a communal garden tended by Old Brown in his dusty bowler hat who mowed the grass and then went to ground in the tool-shed – a safe haven where I kept the rabbit I had been given for my birthday. Daily, it escaped through the bars of its hutch and could usually be found sampling the lettuces on a nearby allotment.

All the local tradesmen's vehicles were horse-drawn. The milkman, the coalman, the baker, the dustman, all had to leave their horses and carts outside in Swains Lane and make their journeys round the village on foot. We got to know the horses well – some we could feed with apple cores, others we wisely left alone. The drying-green was the favourite playground for the children. Though its purpose was for drying the villagers' washing it was more in use as a small patch of grassland for all our outdoor activities.

Indoors, I played with my box of Lotts' bricks and my toy soldiers. However, I never treated my soldiers as warriors and set them up in battle array. Instead, they were ordinary people who just happened to be wearing uniforms.

Our house was small and comfortable. I remember the elderly piano with silk covered front and candlesticks. Another candle in my bedroom; the gas didn't reach all the upstairs rooms although it certainly extended to the spluttering geyser in the small bedroom converted into a bathroom.

Now that Dad was dead, Mum became the bread-winner and joined the staff of the Banque Belge in the city. I started school, aged six, at the Convent in Highgate Road and went back to the Killars' house at number 4 for tea every school day as Mum didn't get home until the evening.

I'm not sure whether I learned very much during my eighteen months at the convent. I could read fairly well before I started there as I began my earliest lessons while staying in Cornwall. For spelling, I had a book with a picture of an object above the printed word; Aunt Kate told me later that she came across me learning my spelling, saying "M-U-G – Cup. MUG – Cup."

Various things stick in my memory from those early days. On winter evenings while we were having tea, we watched the lamp-lighter making his way along Swains Lane with his pole over his shoulder, the lamps lighting up first in the distance, then nearer as he came down the hill past the village. Then there were the horse-drawn funeral processions, passing by on their way to Highgate Cemetery; slow-paced *corteges*, not only to preserve the dignity of the occasions but also because the hill leading up to the cemetery gates was so steep that the jet-black horses were hard put to it to reach the top.

One memory seems hardly credible but I'm sure I'm not making it up. Sometime before the end of the war I have a recollection of a flock of sheep being driven up Swains Lane – a recollection reinforced by seeing a sick sheep dropping out of the flock and lying at the roadside. My mother was there and she fetched a pan of water in the hope of reviving the ailing animal. But who would be herding sheep along residential roads of North London in 1918? Could they have been grazing on Parliament Hill, just past the Number 7 tram terminus ("Twopence all the way" to Kentish Town and Holborn?). Possibly.

With Mother being out all day, something had to be done about running the house and looking after me. So Granny and Grandad Smith packed up their home in Ross-on-Wye and moved into No.5

Holly Village.

Grandad Smith took charge of my out-of-school education in a big way. I would much rather have been outside playing with Joyce and Tim, but Grandad kept me indoors with my nose to the grindstone. Quite right, too, but I didn't think so at the time. By modern standards his methods were somewhat dated. Was it useful? I'm not sure. I can still tell you how many farthings there are, or were, to the pound and various equivalents of ounces, gills, square yards and rods, poles or perches.

My writing was terribly untidy. I had a copy-book in which you had to copy well-meaning and improving maxims... Make hay while the sun shines (pretty obvious)... procrastination is the thief of time (incomprehensible to a seven-year-old).

Copying the copper-plate in ink was tedious. You had to press hard on the down strokes which, apart from blots and smudges, was not too difficult; but on the thin upstrokes the nib splayed and stuck into the paper, showering a fine spray over the pages. The problem of crossed nibs and inconvenient inkwells remained with me for a long time. Even when later I graduated to fountain pens, with dodgy nibs, I was always reluctant to put pen to paper if I could avoid it (I am writing this in ball-point).

I sometimes used to wonder how anyone ever had the patience to write a book. All those words, all those pages! Yet when I found myself doing this for a living, it didn't seem such a sweat after all. I found I actually enjoyed writing a book... so, good old Grandad! All is forgiven!

It was my aunt Margery who took me to my first "grown-up" theatre production. Before that, my godmother, May Thomas, a fellow graduate of my mother's at Aberystwyth had taken me to see *Peter Pan, Where The Rainbow Ends, Treasure Island* and a farce called *The Private Secretary*. This last epic was a corny piece of theatre featuring a typical stage curate of unbelievable naivety who spent most of the time in various subterfuges in order to escape detection. Thus the line "If we are discovered we are lost" produced the riposte "On the contrary, if we are discovered we are found."

I laughed so much I fell off my seat. I mention this as an example of my appreciation of comedy at the age of nine. My critical faculties have, I hope, improved since then.

I was also taken to the London Palladium by Grandma Buckeridge – a most enjoyable outing and commemorated by a pencilled entry in my schoolboys' diary for 1921. It reads "Went to the pleadum."

Later, when Aunt Margery offered to take me to the theatre, she was surprised that instead of opting for something like *Charley's Aunt*, I chose the *Merchant of Venice* with Sybil Thorndike and Lewis Casson as Portia and Shylock at the Lyric Theatre, Hammersmith. It was this production that gave me a love of the theatre which has stayed with me ever since.

It was time now to consider what was to be done about my education. Had my father survived the war I should probably have gone to my father's old school, William Ellis, a North London day grammar school. I would certainly not have been sent to boarding school, for the Buckeridge family would never have subscribed to the hierarchical tradition of sending children away to school to have their rough corners rubbed off and thereby moulded into potential members of the conservative establishment. Rather the reverse! We have always belonged to the lower middle strata of society. One grandfather was a solicitor's clerk, the other a village schoolmaster. My mother was the first member of the family to go to a university.

However, my father as I have said worked in a bank and after the war a charitable organisation called the Bank Clerks' Orphanage scooped up most of the fatherless children of the bank employees who had not survived and undertook to pay for their education at a number of independent boarding schools. I was to be sent to Seaford College in Sussex, thereby allowing my mother to continue working for her living with fewer domestic responsibilities.

What was a boarding school? Tommy Killar told me it was a place where you had to sleep on boards instead of beds. (In the event, he wasn't so far out in his prophecy) Joyce thought it meant a Board School; this didn't sound too promising either as there was a Board School, i.e. an elementary school run by the Board of Education which we walked past on our way to the Archway Road. When the windows were open you could hear forty or so juvenile voices chanting in unison "I-C-E – Ice, B-U-N – Bun." But I knew that already, along with M-U-G – Cup, which I had now long discarded. Indeed, I could now read fluently and spell fairly well, thanks to Grandad Smith.

2

Seaford College had been founded by a Colonel Savage in 1884. In 1920, when I arrived, it had been taken over by the Rev. L. Stanley Cowan, a large man with a florid complexion and a forthright manner of speech.

At that time there were about 70 boarders of which we Bank Boys were a small minority. Conditions were primitive to start with but, to his credit, Cowan started to improve his property, erecting new buildings and installing modern plumbing during the next few years.

He began by replacing the stinking bog which greeted us upon arrival. It consisted of three buckets beneath the holed-out seats, which had to be emptied every day by the school odd-job man. There must have been better toilet facilities elsewhere for the staff, but we couldn't think where they could be – which gave rise to the theory of one seven-year old amongst us who decided that masters were an exclusive species who never needed to go to the lavatory.

In my dormitory we had three wash basins, but only one jug of water. When this ran out, as it sometimes did, those in the lower pecking order, to which I belonged, had to wash in the water already used by the more privileged members of the dormitory.

The food, in the early days, was unappetising and there was never enough of it! Two slices of bread and margarine for tea was little enough to sustain a hungry eight-year-old until breakfast next morning. I still remember the agonised expression of a boy sent out from tea for some misdemeanour before he had even started his frugal ration. His face appeared outside the dining-hall window imploring us, by frantic lip-reading, to smuggle out something to stave off his hunger during the night. I did on one occasion manage to conceal a slice of bread under my jersey to eat after lights-out, but I got caught while trying to undress under Matron's all-seeing eye. She was quite nice about it; I had to eat the dry bread for breakfast next morning, but she didn't pursue the matter further than that.

Not that breakfast was much to look forward to. After a thin porridge we spread our own preserves, supplied from home, on bread known as toak (possibly derived from toque, a durable material for making women's hats). I took a 1lb pot of jam, marmalade and golden syrup back with me each term, but they never lasted the thirteen weeks my mother had intended them for. Having reached the bottom of each jar the custom was to award three of your friends with the scrapings. Needless to say "third scrapings" was a meaningless entitlement to wipe the stickiness from the sides of the jar.

I also took a home-made cake back with me each term. While it lasted, which wasn't long, you could reward your friends and buy off your enemies with promises and threats: "I'll cross you off my cake list, if you don't watch out."

We had our birthday cakes sent from home; these wonderful confections of icing and marzipan were the ultimate reward or threat to anyone hoping for a slice. There was, however, a terrible disaster one day when a boy, whose name escapes me, took his birthday cake up to the master on duty to ask for permission to take the cake, already sliced, to his friends at other tables.

It so happened that the headmaster had made one of his rare appearances in the dining-hall and was chatting to the matron and master on duty at the top table. The boy (it could have been Woodhams or Doyle or possibly Walters) stood behind the master awaiting an opportunity to make his request.

The headmaster turned and saw the boy waiting patiently at his elbow. "Ah, Woodhams! (or Doyle or possibly Walters) Is that for me? How kind of you." He then took a slice and treated himself to a bite. "A beautiful cake! Don't you agree, Matron?"

Matron couldn't say, not having tried it, so she had to be offered a slice – so, too, did the master on duty. Walters (or Woodhams *et al*) stood paralysed with horror as three precious slices disappeared down the throats of adults who should have known better.

After the meal, Woodhams (or whoever) was confronted by three furious cake-less claimants thwarted of their expectations by this outrageous act of sabotage.

"What did you want to give them your cake for?" they demanded.

"I couldn't help it. They all took a bit."

"Why didn't you tell them it wasn't meant for them?"

"Huh! All very well for you to talk. I'd like to see *you* tell them."

At the age of nine the prospect of standing up for your rights in confrontation with headmasters entangles the vocal chords in clove-hitches of apprehension… the words just won't come.

Apart from the headmaster and his married brother-in-law, the rest of the staff consisted of recently-demobbed junior army officers who were trying their hand at teaching as an alternative to running a chicken farm; I doubt whether they had much in the way of teaching qualifications. They came and went almost before you had the chance to get to know them, arriving and leaving at odd times during the term and seldom reappearing after the following holidays. I don't know whether they were sacked or left of their own accord, but only one or two stayed for a full academic year. A few were small-scale tyrants but most were easy-going and would, if encouraged, spend a whole lesson telling us about their exploits during the war. The lowest form was taught by a succession of mistresses. They, too, came and went rather quickly.

One master I liked very much was an out-of-work actor (Mr Saville), who organised school entertainments on end-of-pier concert party lines. These were my happiest moments, as I enjoyed acting and though by far the youngest member of the troupe (the rest were about 16 or 17) I was always allowed to perform what I hoped was a comic item. There were set-backs, of course; once I spent the whole of the Easter holidays copying out and learning one of W.S.Gilbert's *Bab Ballads* only to be told on returning to school the following term that a senior boy had decided to perform the item – so that was that! Even so, I can still, after 75 years, recite Gilbert's *Etiquette* without a prompt. I was sorry when Mr Saville left. Like the others, he just quit the scene without explanation.

Mr Saville's concerts may not have been of high artistic quality, but they were all we had, for the Arts were not well represented at this time. We had no library, no orchestra, no art lessons and no drama. There was no music except for the odd ukulele banjo and there were times when we were hard pressed to find anyone capable of playing the hymn for morning assembly. My mother had paid for me to have piano lessons, but in the absence of an adult music teacher I was taught by a senior boy (F.A.Dunn) who was a good pianist and an exception to the rule of limited musicality. Sheet music was in short supply so Dunn taught me to play *Loving Shepherd of Thy Sheep* (no 334 in *Hymns Ancient and Modern*). I had learnt it by heart after the first lesson and, knowing the correct chords, I used to play other tunes by ear. I developed a wide repertoire – but only in the key of D!

The number of boys was slowly increasing, despite the fact that quite a few of them (like the staff) didn't stay for very long. Mr Cowan continued to improve his property by, for example, draining out low-lying playing fields. Maybe this left him little time for teaching, for he seldom appeared in the classroom. The only time I can remember him taking a lesson with our form was the day before officials from the Board of Education were due to inspect the school. On this occasion the headmaster came into our classroom, taught a brilliant, prepared lesson and plied us with questions to which he made sure that we knew the correct answers. Next day, when the inspector was present, he came in and repeated the previous day's lesson, almost word for word, taking care to ask us the same questions with which we had been primed the day before. The inspector was impressed and went away satisfied. We were told that the school was now recognised by the Board of Education.

Conditions improved. We now had a tuck-shop, a science lab and a cadet corps; the latter, however, didn't survive the General Strike of 1926, for the authorities, alarmed at our possession of lethal weapons (or fearing riots at a time of crisis), swooped down on us and confiscated our small stock of rifles and out-of-date carbines.

The cadet corps, while it lasted, was a popular alternative to compulsory games. We had field exercises consisting of mock attacks on neighbouring villages.

Our assault on the village of Bishopstone was particularly noteworthy. The previous Sunday the school had attended Matins there as an alternative to our usual attendance at St Leonard's, Seaford. While reading the lesson, the vicar stopped and said, "If the boy at the back doesn't stop laughing, I shall cancel the service."

This untimely breach of good manners on the part of the school obviously called for an apology. So, after our field exercise at Bishopstone a few days later, the cadet corps, with fixed bayonets and led by a sword-bearing officer, marched up to the vicarage and presented arms outside the front door. The vicar upon emerging was visibly taken aback. Did he imagine he was facing a firing squad? However, he recovered his composure on hearing that we had come to apologise.

On another occasion, when we were planning to infiltrate the village of Alfriston, one over-zealous cadet swam across the River Cuckmere and spent an unhappy, tooth-chattering afternoon in his sodden uniform.

The boys in the mid-1920s were a social and ethnic mix. Well-heeled parents provided sons who were not quite clever enough to make the grade for entrance to a public school; others were colonials from various outposts of Empire. We had boys from pretty well everywhere in the world. There was never the slightest question raised about colour or creed. Political correctness didn't exist. The foreigners answered cheerfully to racial nicknames which would be unthinkable today. Nobody took offence because none was intended.

One Indian boy was the son of a Rajah. I was sorry for him because his religion obliged him to bathe every day and on freezing cold February mornings he could be seen shivering under the cold shower in the draughty annexe just off the changing room.

The standard of education was slow to improve. As the foreigners had no need to take examinations and many of the English couldn't have passed them anyway, few among the masters made much attempt to lead us on to dizzy heights of academic brilliance.

The exception was C Melville-Hockin, who arrived in the middle 20s. He was a splendid schoolmaster and the only member of staff to survive the transfer to the new regime when Cowan sold the school to an educational trust in 1928.

As Cowan's little empire expanded, his interest in the day-to-day running of the school decreased. He no longer took classes, never appeared for morning assembly and never ate with the school in the dining-hall. He left the running of the daily routine to his brother-in-law (H.P.Hamilton) who, in turn, left it to the master on duty who, in turn, left it to the prefects who, thanks to Hockin, kept the routine ticking over pretty well.

A few clever boys took their studies seriously and were entered for School Certificate but, in the main, there was a tendency to do as little schoolwork as you could get away with. This was encouraged, in part, by volunteering to work as an unpaid navvy on improvements being carried out in the school grounds – improvements which added a great deal to the value of the property. During my time, the low-lying playing fields were drained, tennis courts constructed and landscaping carried out, using chalk boulders filched from the foreshore a hundred yards away. The headmaster's working parties could often serve as an excuse for not going into class – sometimes for days on end.

Somewhat to my surprise, I was included in a group of potentially promising exam candidates. We did not attend normal classes but were expected to work on our own without a timetable or any formal teaching by a master. The result was that members of the group spent the time in studying the subjects they enjoyed the most and neglecting the others.

I read and re-read the Shakespeare plays of which we had the texts. When the self-tutoring scheme was eventually abandoned I had absorbed a knowledge of Shakespeare which has stayed in my mind ever since, but I have forgotten most of what I had ever learned of French, Latin, Physics and Maths.

Our confirmation classes were taken by the local curate (J.Tyler Whittle), but on the day before we were confirmed there was an unvarying ritual. One by one the candidates were summoned to the HM's study for a man-to-man initiation into the world of human sexuality, of which it was tacitly assumed that we knew nothing. The proceedings went like this:

"Well, Buckeridge, you are growing up now. I don't suppose you know how you were born, do you?"

"No, sir." This was the obligatory reply.

"It's like this. When a mother and father decide to start a family, the man passes the seed to the woman, and in the course of time a child is born. Any questions?"

"No, sir."

"Right! Send the next boy in."

I went out trying to visualise a highly-coloured packet of sunflower seeds being handed from husband to wife across the dining-room table.

We were always wary of Mr Cowan's rather forbidding manner and did our best to keep out of his way. However, he could be jovial, indeed genial, when he felt like it; and, with hindsight, I feel that our opinion of him was unduly harsh. The reverend gentleman certainly had his kindly moments. On one occasion, at the end of term, the school had permission to go to the local cinema. I was shifting a wheelbarrow of turf for the nearly-completed tennis court when a master came round taking names of those wishing to go.

Mr Cowan, who had arrived to inspect the new tennis court, noticed that I was the only boy who had declined the duty-master's invitation. He asked me why and I explained that I had no money.

"Put Buckeridge on the list," he boomed in forthright tones to the master on duty. "I will pay for his ticket."

So he couldn't *really* have been such a monster after all!

Our new headmaster was the Rev J.S.MacNutt who came to us from Canford School. Despite speculation on our part, we never knew what internal politics by the governing body resulted in Mr MacNutt's apparent relegation from being Head of a large school with a good reputation to becoming Head of a small school with, at that time, very little reputation at all; but we sought consolation in the fact that Seaford was founded in 1884 whereas Canford was not established until 1923. However, Canford's loss was Seaford's gain.

The Rev J.S.MacNutt was as different from his predecessor as chalk from cheese. He was a tall, upright figure with a reserved manner and a dignity which he never allowed to let slip in public, though in private conversation he could be affable, indeed charming. I grew to like him very much in my last two years, though to begin with he scared the living daylights out of me. His was a bachelor's world, underlined by his appearance. His Guard's-style moustache – unusual among parsons in those days – emphasized his masculinity. You never saw him in casual clothes or with his jacket unbuttoned. He was, indeed, a buttoned-up person. He was certainly narrow-minded, and censored – with scissors, occasionally – the magazines and newspapers we were allowed to read. In my last year, when I was Head of School, I sat next to him daily at the lunch table. Conversation was politely constrained; he curtly discouraged any small-talk that might arise concerning the female sex, alcohol or gambling.

By today's standards he was racist in his views about the superiority of England and the English. Finding that the school he had taken over contained a small number of what he called "half-castes" he set about gently getting rid of them and not taking any more. We ended up a hundred per cent White.

He was certainly generous. In 1929, when I was due to leave, he invited me back for a further school year without charging my mother any fees.

For this, and other things, I shall be eternally grateful to J.S. MacNutt.

3

I went back to our London home in the school holidays for the first few years of the Twenties. My school friend, Val Guest, who later became a film director, lived in Finchley Road and I spent a fair amount of time in his flat. His father had a small chocolate factory which was an added inducement for a visit.

It was quite common in those days for children to travel around London by themselves without coming to any harm. To visit Val I took the train from Gospel Oak station to Finchley Road and did the rest of the journey on foot. Unsupervised, I went shopping for my grandmother, walked to Camden Town to visit Uncle Arthur and his wife Ruby, and sometimes (not often, as it meant spending money) to the pictures in the Archway Road with the Killar children.

Our doctor, Alfred Slate, was a relation on my father's side of the family. He was elderly (or seemed so to me) and lived in Canonbury NW. He visited his patients on foot or by public transport and was probably the last doctor in London to be seen going on his rounds by tram while wearing a top hat.

One year, before I went to boarding school, my grandparents took me to Broadstairs for a fortnight. My mum couldn't come as she was working. I have vague recollections of afternoon excursions to Margate and Canterbury, but for most of the time I followed my favourite pastime of sitting cross-legged on Broadstairs sands listening to Uncle Mack's Minstrels of blacked-up entertainers performing twice daily on their stage beside the sea. They played banjos, piano and percussion and possibly other instruments as well, and sang songs such as *I'm Forever Blowing Bubbles* and *Yes, We Have No Bananas.* I thought they were marvellous. What need of buckets and spades and shrimping-nets with this cultural (almost) concert to be had twice daily free of charge.

A little research about Uncle Mack revealed that he started his busking career on the sands in 1895. Later, he formed his troupe at Broadstairs, which he ran for forty years without a break.

But that wasn't the end of Mack. After World War 2, when Sylvia and I were living in Ramsgate (I was teaching at St Lawrence College at the time), we took Sally and Tim to Broadstairs and there was the avuncular busker still strumming his banjo. He no longer had minstrels and was performing solo at an indoor theatre.

Children were invited to go on stage and perform. Tim, aged six, in Chinese fancy dress costume complete with drooping black moustache, mounted the stage and sang *Chin Chin Chinaman* – or as much of it as he could remember, for I have a memory of Sally going up to help him out in the last verse. Nobody realised at that time that it was politically incorrect to sing a song poking fun at a stereotype Chinaman.

For the next two summer holidays we spent a week or two in Brighton, staying at friends of my grandparents. Mum joined us at weekends whenever she could but was never able to fix her holidays to coincide with the Brighton fortnight.

Brighton Beach was little different from our pebbly foreshore at Seaford, except that it was more crowded, so it was away from the water's edge that I looked for a diversion.

I didn't have far to look. Jack Shepherd's Entertainers were performing thrice daily in the open-air theatre facing the promenade, and that's where I spent a lot of my time – not within the enclosure where you had to pay to go in, but with my nose pressed against the railings where you could see and hear the performance for nothing; the only contribution was a penny, if you happened to have one, in the collecting box when the "bottler" came round.

The old-style Pierrot costume was on its way out and Jack Shepherd's Entertainers wore blazers and flannels with straw boaters. I can't remember what the ladies wore, but they too had foresworn the traditional ruff and pom-poms. The performances were reasonably varied though not, as claimed, changed at every performance. But for me, attending on the outskirts twice daily (I wasn't allowed to stay up for the evening bash) I soon knew every song, sketch and joke by heart. I could have prompted if anyone had fluffed his lines.

Years later (when I was about fifteen) we went on holiday to Llandudno where to my joy I discovered an open-air Pierrot theatre in the Happy Valley. Once again, I was wont to haunt the railing twice (or sometimes thrice) daily.

The only other time I can remember going away on holiday in those early years was at the age of seven or eight. Mum took me with her to an Old Students' reunion at Aberystwyth where she had been an undergraduate. Also present was my Aunt Billy, a fellow undergrad with Mum, and her daughter Daphne, three days older than me. I was given a shilling to take Daphne to a café on the promenade and ply her with drink (lemonade actually). This I did and sat through our refreshment break in an agony of apprehension though Daphne, the invited guest, had no qualms. What would happen if the bill came to more than a shilling? What on earth would I say? Would I be arrested? Thrown out? Made to do the washing up? All was well; the bill came to eightpence.

Aberystwyth seemed very carefree and liberal, though I remember Mum telling me later that when she had been at Aber the women students were, as a great concession, allowed to attend debates in the men's union provided they walked there in a supervised, two-by-two crocodile and refrained from speaking to any male students whom they might encounter. That was in 1901; I expect it's different now!

In 1923 Grandad Smith died. He must have been ailing for some time but I was unaware of this and it came as a shock to me, away at boarding school, to open my eagerly-awaited letter from home and be confronted with this sad news.

Shortly afterwards Granny Smith became ill and went into hospital for an operation which gave her a further ten years to live.

She survived on an unappetising diet of fish boiled in milk; in time I got used to the smell.

Granny Smith had never liked living in London and, after Grandad died, Mum changed her job. 5 Holly Village was sold and we moved to the country – or rather to a satellite town in Hertfordshire where Mum had been offered a post which rejoiced in the enigmatic name of Hospitality Secretary to the recently-formed Garden City Company.

Welwyn Garden City had been rising from the mud and turning Ebenezer Howard's dream into a reality since 1920.

Already a great deal had been done. When we arrived early in 1924 Welwyn Stores – the only shop – was built and in business. There were even bi-weekly silent film shows at the Kinema in an adjoining hall.

Temporary huts for offices and accommodation for building workers were dotted about, houses were sprouting along the verges of emerging roads, and a narrow-gauge railway with tractors pulling tons of bricks was delivering material to the house-builders. The main line railway station had not been started, but a platform had been erected alongside the branch line from Luton. Journeys to London involved changing trains at Hatfield. But there was mud everywhere!

It was a time of growth based on idealistic and almost unbelievable faith. Ebenezer Howard and his like-minded pioneers faced serious financial setbacks as they strove to turn their dream into reality. Sir Theodore Chambers, the chairman of the company, wrote, "The real truth was that no-one believed in the future of the town. Everyone, even our friends, was utterly sceptical."

But nothing daunted Ebenezer. I remember him as a little old man in his seventies with a white moustache and a black raincoat, striding around the building sites. His brilliant architect, Louis de Soissons, and his faithful disciple, Frederick Osborn, were never far behind.

Mum's job was difficult to define; she did everything. New residents were arriving daily and Mum was the fount of information to which they turned. She made sure that their houses were ready for habitation; her duties ranged from ordering their coal to booking seats for them at London theatres. A book of cartoons *Who's What In Welwyn* published a few years later shows Mum at her desk above the caption:

> *"From Petersfield to Puckeridge*
> *The world knows Mrs Buckeridge,*
> *Good information daily pours*
> *From Mrs B at Welwyn Stores."*

Not immortal verse, perhaps, but it sums up her job pretty well.

These were the days before the arrival of the factories, though they weren't far away. A large hoarding in a field beside the railway announced *Seven Acre Site for Shredded Wheat*. Coming shortly were ICI, Murphy Radio, Cresta Silks, Nivea Cream, Bickie-pegs and the Film Studio (British Instructional Films) where I made my debut on the silver screen in a production of Ernest Raymond's *Tell England!* directed by Anthony Asquith. I have to admit that my part didn't qualify for star billing; I was merely one of the spectators at a school swimming match. I got other walk-on parts in later films but they didn't amount to very much.

For the first few months after our arrival, Mum rented a house in Handside Lane while she reviewed the housing situation. She settled on 11 Russellcroft Road, costing I think £1100. Electric light was a novelty after the gas lighting of Holly Village. Our garden was about the size of a tennis court – rather too large, I sometimes felt, as it was my job to mow and roll the grass when I was at home.

It was about this time (1924) that Mum bought me my first bike. My enthusiasm was sparked off by a neighbour, Fitzwater Wray, who was a cycling journalist for the national newspapers. He wrote under the name of Kuklos (Greek – a wheel). My bicycle, built to his specification, was low and light in weight as opposed to the traditional shop models (chain-guards, mounting-steps, sit-up-and-beg handlebars), which had hardly changed in design for fifty years. Cycling became my chief hobby for some years after I had outgrown my Kuklos model and, in later holidays, when I was about sixteen, I cycled as much as a hundred miles in one day. I must admit I only achieved this figure twice, and the first time, after a 6am start and a tour round the neighbouring counties, I got home with the cyclometer on the front wheel registering a disappointing 98.5 miles. This wasn't good enough so I went on riding round the local roads until the magic figure was achieved.

Later I joined a cycling club and went riding with them during the school holidays; not very often, though, because I couldn't afford the large café teas that were traditional at the end of a Sunday a-wheel.

I used to enjoy helping at the road races which took place early on Sunday mornings during the summer. Helping, or watching, involved getting up at four o'clock in the morning and riding off to somewhere like Baldock or St Neot's where the race would be starting on some quiet stretch of country road.

Road racing in the twenties never allowed a bunched start of riders competing for places, for racing on the King's highway was illegal. Instead, there were time trials with the competitors starting off at one-minute intervals. The riders had to be clothed from neck to ankle (no bare knees or elbows in the 20s) so the rule was to wear black tights like dancers in a corps-de-ballet with a skimpy black jacket.

My great friend at the time was Doug Rudd, an American, whose father had come to the UK from California to work on starting up the Shredded Wheat Company. Doug was a keen Scout so naturally I joined the movement and became a member of his patrol.

Opposition to my joining was voiced by Granny Smith because of the cost of the uniform. This came to 25 shillings (£1.25) and was good value, consisting, as it did, of shirt, shorts, hat, belt, socks, neckerchief and various trimmings. Eventually, with Mum's support, I wore down the opposition, but the problem of expense reared its head whenever any sort of purchase was mooted. Admittedly, we had very little money, but even so, Granny was terrified of spending a penny if she could avoid it.

She was, of course, a mid-Victorian, born in 1856 when penury was the nightmare of the genteel working and lower middle classes. Not for them the unemployment benefit, the National Health Service and all the advantages of a welfare state. Then, it was charity or the workhouse if you couldn't afford to eat. It was, remember, not so long since debtors (*cf* Charles Dickens' father) could be sent to prison until a debt had been discharged.

So, Rule One for most of the earning classes had been "He who went a-borrowing went a-sorrowing." While on the topic of Victorian rhymed aphorisms, here's another one:

> *"Naughty little curse words*
> *Hang, Dash and Blow*
> *These and other worse words*
> *Will send you Down Below!"*

The early residents of Welwyn had to put up with the benevolently mocking reputation of being a bunch of bearded, sandal-shod vegetarian fanatics in home-spun clothes – the 20s equivalent of woolly-hatted *Guardian* readers. Certainly, there were some eccentrics, but most of the new people had come to Welwyn Garden City knowing that they would find themselves among like-minded neighbours keen on living in a different sort of town and a different sort of environment.

A few Labour MPs came to live in the town; there was a good sprinkling of artists, musicians, writers (with Bernard Shaw not far off in Ayot St Lawrence), but what I chiefly remember was the interest in drama. It was only a small town but we had four or five drama clubs producing first at the Parkway Hall and later at the Barn Theatre.

The first time I saw Flora Robson on stage (she wasn't a Dame in those days – she was working at the office of the Shredded Wheat factory) was in a rather corny comedy called *The Dippers* at the Parkway Hall. I don't remember much about the play, but I'll never forget Flora – she shone!

I couldn't do any acting while still at school but, from the time I left and was working at the bank, acting with the Folk Players, the Theatre Society or the Thalians became more than a hobby. Besides all this activity the manager of the newly-built cinema occasionally put on a one-act play as part of the entertainment. I was cast in a play by Miles Malleson and we performed between the Pathe Gazette news reel and the main film. I got somewhat tired of the news reel by the end of the week.

Then, in 1931, came the Barn Theatre. This was originally a cowshed at Handside Farm and adapted with enthusiasm by the local drama clubs. It is still going strong and is one of the prestigious Little Theatres of the nationwide Little Theatre organisation.

But way back at the turn of the decade the Christmas carol-singers had the option of adapting *Once In Royal David's City* to a topical theme.

"Once in Welwyn Garden City
Stood a lowly cattle shed
Till a dedicated actor
Said "Let's have a theatre instead."
Praise and thanks to the creator
Of the Welwyn Barn The-atre."

Author – Anon!

We no longer had to use the Parkway Hall, for the Barn was suitable for most productions. But for really large productions – and the Thalians regularly staged full-scale musicals – it was necessary to buy out the superbly-equipped cinema.

The cinema was also taken over by the annual drama festival. Teams from all over the country competed in the farrago of twenty-four one-act plays. Four plays a night for a week – quite a marathon for the enthusiastic thespians. Even so, the festival was always a sell-out.

4

Everybody said that I was lucky to get a job in the bank (where my father had worked) when I left school in July 1930. In one sense they were right. The City was still staggering from the effects of the Wall Street Crash of the previous year when so many city organisations went bankrupt. Unemployment was high and here I was being offered a permanent, safe job in a bank that paid your income tax and gave you a good pension when you finally retired.

Doubtless, it was a good job, offering splendid opportunities to the right person. But I was not the right person. I was 18 and the retirement age of 65 was so far into the future that I was not prepared to spend my working life waiting for a comfortable pension to come along in due course.

I did try for a short time to see myself as a City gent (though I drew the line at wearing a bowler hat, an emblem that my colleagues seemed to find indispensable). I even studied for bank exams and succeeded in passing them; but it was no good. I didn't know what it was all about.

In my innocence/ignorance I had thought of a bank as a friendly sort of social club where Mr Bones, the butcher, and Mr Bun, the baker, popped in to deposit the day's takings or borrow the odd tenner when he was running short... It is not like that! Complicated details involving stocks and shares, mortgages, executors, trustees, nominees, powers of attorney and foreign exchange were all happening very fast in the higher reaches of the organisation. Fortunately I was thrown in at the shallow end where these frightening concepts didn't concern me but remained the unseen menace of the future.

I was directed to the branch at Kings Cross where the staff were friendly and helpful, and they needed to be for one so ignorant as I was. Passbooks in those days were entered up in ink, and my job was to enter the daily transactions in the correct columns. That was easy but there were rare occasions when I put figures in the wrong column, generously awarding customers sums which should have been deducted – and vice versa. However I devised a foolproof method to prevent debits and credits going astray; it is a method which you are unlikely to find in any orthodox manual about banking and economics. It says "*The debit side is the side nearest the window.*"

After entering up the passbooks I had to cope with the remittances which consisted of the cashiers on the counter deluging me with cheques to be sorted into banking groups and totted up. By the end of the day this figure was in thousands of pounds and the total had to agree with the cashiers' own figure. If it didn't agree (which was frequently), I had to do my sums all over again. There was an old adding machine but nobody used it as the mechanical lever-operated process took longer than the adding up of pounds, shillings and pence by mental arithmetic.

On December 31st everything had to be totalled and balanced to provide the final financial figures for the whole year. This meant working until midnight for all of us, and to alleviate the strain (or the monotony) various colleagues brought in quantities of alcohol to see them through the evening. They passed the bottles around in generous measure, so well before midnight struck I could barely see the window let alone which side was debit and which credit. Fortunately, the Bank survived the financial shock.

The most frustrating part of working for the Bank was being cooped up all day. I envied the customers as they came and went; they at least were free to walk about in the streets for a short time.

Occasionally, however, a couple of juniors would be sent as messengers to some other branch that needed more cash. The money was supposed to be carried in a stout leather bag, but we devised the ploy of stuffing thousands of pounds in notes into our trouser pockets and trailing the bag along as visible bait to any bag-snatchers that we might encounter. We rather hoped that the bag would indeed be snatched, thus rewarding us with the last laugh. But this never happened; perhaps the bag-snatchers (if any) had rumbled our ingenious(?) ruse. This of course was in the halcyon days before we had armoured security vans on the streets. I doubt whether Securicor staff stuff their trouser pockets with old bank notes as they go about their business.

I joined a hockey club and played on Saturday afternoons, when I got away from the bank in time, for in my day bank staff worked on Saturday mornings. At school I had been in the first XI hockey team and also in the first XV rugger team. My cricket was pretty useless, brought on, I always claim, not so much by my lack of cohesion between hand and eye, but by an incident that occurred when at about the age of eleven I was picked to play in a junior team against a local prep school. Proud and confident, I strode to the wicket to face the bowling – and was bowled out first ball. The shock, shame and humiliation ate into my soul so that for ever after when playing cricket I always faced the first ball with apprehension and dread.

I gave up rugger, too, when I left school. I think my place in the team depended upon my speed as a wing three-quarter. I hated the kick and rush tactics of the forward line and the resultant pile-up of writhing legs and bodies when the scrum collapsed. At wing three-quarter, I was spared much of the hurly-burly. But hockey was a game where violent body collisions did not occur and at right wing I went on playing hockey until my forties.

On some Saturdays, while at the bank, the match would be cancelled so, being in the City, I went to a matinee at the Old Vic or Sadlers Wells. It was a time when actors such as Ralph Richardson or Robert Speight were the leading performers in the Shakespeare plays at these theatres. Not always, however, with much of an audience. One foggy November day when hockey was cancelled I went to the Old Vic and saw *Hamlet* in its four-hour entirety. There were just two of us in the gallery (admission 6d). I had a front row seat but my fellow drama enthusiast didn't take a seat at all. He spent the entire four hours standing in the gangway under a feeble emergency light, following the script word by word in his copy of the play. I don't think he ever once looked to see what was happening on stage.

During my last year at school I had, in a spirit of misplaced machismo, taken up boxing. The result was that my nose was not exactly broken, but various bones had been chipped and knocked out of shape. It wasn't painful but it rather spoiled the nasal symmetry. So after work one evening I went to the ENT hospital in Grays Inn Road to see if they could do anything about it. There the matter rested for some weeks during which my annual holiday was fixed. I had booked to go to Lucerne (my first time abroad) and shortly before I was due to go I was summoned to hospital for the beautifying nose job. As this would involve only a local anaesthetic I knew that I should be discharged before my holiday was due to start three days later. The minor operation went ahead according to schedule but, on the third day following, problems ensued. Mum was taking Granny to Aberystwyth. I saw them off at Welwyn and followed later as far as London.Very soon I began to feel ill. I went back to the hospital and told them that I was due to travel overnight to Switzerland. The doctor told me I would be mad to do any such thing. By now I felt so ill that I had to agree with him and reluctantly phoned the travel company to cancel my reservation.

I made a fairly quick recovery. Indeed, two days later I felt fine and, having now lost my booking in Lucerne, I decided to join Mum in Wales.

After a fortnight, I returned to the ENT hospital. My left ear was suppurating and I was clearly suffering from mastoiditis brought on by septicaemia from the first operation. However, I survived and spent a few weeks in the same ward where I had my nose operation. In 1931, there was no NHS; meals were basic and we had to provide extras for ourselves, rather like boarding school. We spent a lot of time rolling bandages, which after being boiled were used again and again – unless they were too bloody for general use.

My convalescence lasted for four months. (How did the bank survive without my expertise?) When at last I returned to work I was transferred to the Registrar's department in Old Broad Street. This was tedious but easy (no hard sums to get wrong). I merely had to record the buying and selling of bank shares and enter the names of the customers in the most chaotic address book anyone could imagine.

I was, however, getting restless. I had always wanted to be a teacher and I started working out how this could best be done. I had been left £500 in the will of Mr E.A.Symons, a friend and bank colleague of my father. This was to enable me to take a degree at Oxford, where an ancestor, Bishop Buckeridge, had been a co-founder in the 16th Century of St John's College. But, owing to inflation after World War One, it was decided that although the legacy would have seen me through two years at Oxford it just wasn't enough to sustain a final year. I decided to go to University College, London, instead. It turned out to be an unwise decision.

I wanted to read English, but I had dropped Latin at school and Latin was compulsory for an Arts degree. I also needed London Matric in five subjects, so I took the exam, studying in the evenings at Birkbeck College, taking Physics in place of Latin which I could do later on as a separate subject. This worked out well. I passed my Matric in five subjects and was accepted for University College on the condition that I passed in Latin at a later date. At Birkbeck, I met various students who had come up against the regulations prevailing at the time. One chap had taken the exam five times, passing in four subjects and failing one in a different subject each time. Another had passed in four subjects but failed in Latin each time. So I left the bank and took a junior post in a prep school at Rhyl, where I planned to study for my Latin Matric in my spare time knowing that I had a place at University College for the following year.

It was during my time in Rhyl that I met Sylvia Brown. Her father was a doctor in a mining village called Ffynnon Groew and her mother, Eva, was the younger sister of Emmeline Pankhurst; a fact which I found out later, as Mrs Brown did not comment on her relationship with this illustrious family of whom Christabel and Sylvia were still very much engaged in supporting women's rights.

Dr Brown was a friendly, elderly man who had first qualified as an engineer before turning to medicine. I sometimes accompanied him on his rounds and also to road accidents. There were far fewer cars but the roads had hardly been updated from the days of horse traffic and accidents were frequent on the winding country lanes.

I was often invited to supper at the Browns'; I was more than pleased to accept, for the doctor's household enjoyed a higher standard of living than I had met before; after boarding school fare the suppers were something to look forward to. The doctor's house (with two servants) was an oasis in the midst of a backward mining community. The village had no electricity and no running water.

The doctor's man, Tom, accompanied him on his rounds, acting at times as chauffeur/interpreter in the Welsh-speaking mining villages where the miners walked up to six miles each way to get to and from work. No pit-head baths; they walked home from the valley to the hilltops coated in coal dust.

The doctor had a telephone but it was fairly primitive. It could take incoming calls without problems, but for an outgoing call you had to wind up a generator in order to call the exchange. Plumbing, too, was primitive. The Browns had a rainwater tank which could pump water up to the bathroom (the only one in the village) but, for drinking water, Tom had to carry buckets to the communal well some hundreds of yards away from the house. Oil lamps were in general use. Electricity was on its way, but had not got there in 1933.

I partnered Sylvia at local dances and various social functions. I was pleased to have a girl friend at a platonic level for I had no intention of forming a lasting relationship. But as we were together so much it came to be assumed that ours was a proper engagement. If we did discuss the future together, it was something to be thought about in years to come when I had finished at college and was in a financial position to get married. With such discussions so far in the future, I was naively happy to go along with things as they were. But Sylvia wanted a formal engagement and this was presented to me as a *fait accompli* which at the time I was willing to accept.

For some years the marriage was a happy one. We raised two children, Sally and Tim, whom we both loved dearly. But as the time passed the cracks in our relationship grew wider; Sylvia and I were not compatible and the marriage broke down irretrievably.

5

First year students at University College were advised that however many clubs and societies they might be prevailed upon to join, they should eschew the Dramatic Society as it encroached too much on their periods of study.

I heeded this advice to start with, but my resolution faded when I was asked to play St Francis in the College's traditional production of Lawrence Housman's *Little Plays of St Francis.* This annual production was widely acclaimed and also enjoyed a BBC transmission as the icing on the cake. I should mention that the broadcast had none of the preparation and rehearsal of a radio play in later times. The cast merely went along to Broadcasting House on a Sunday afternoon, ranged themselves haphazardly round a microphone, and went straight into the script without rehearsal.

I joined the hockey club and the Socialist Society. It was the time of Oswald Mosely's fascist marches through London so we duly arranged anti-blackshirt demonstrations against them. Our usual shouted slogan was "Hitler and Mosely mean hunger and war" although Hitler had hardly got into his stride by then. Sometimes our chant was directed against Hitler and Baldwin, though this was perhaps a little hard to Prime Minister "Honest Stan" who was doing his nut trying to keep the peace.

There was a dockstrike and we marched off to the East End of London to give the dockers our support under the dubious shouted slogan of "Workers, students and intellectuals unite!" We were certainly students, but claiming to be "intellectuals" was somewhat over the top. The dockers must have thought so too; they reluctantly came out of the pubs, where they'd been enjoying a well-earned rest from unloading cotton and bananas and stood about amused and derisive at our earnest efforts on their behalf.

There was also the ill-fated Anti-War Society. We went on a Hyde Park demo where our banner, University College Anti-War

Society, was photographed by the press and duly published in one of the glossy magazines – it was either the *Tatler* or the *Illustrated London News*. The name of the College prominently displayed was too much for our Provost. The Society was banned forthwith.

I enjoyed the lectures in English, French and History and worked as well as I was able, but the demon Latin defeated me and, failing badly in this subject, I was unable to go on and take a degree.

I married Sylvia in 1936 and took a teaching job at a prep school in Suffolk. I was sorry for the boys; they were as deprived as I had been at their age and had no facilities worth talking about. The headmaster was a reasonable man but his wife was a harridan who frightened the life out of boys and staff (including her husband). She would burst into a classroom, disrupting a lesson to complain of some triviality, or shout through the dining-room hatch because some luckless pupil hadn't eaten the mustard on his plate. Further examples of this woman's behaviour are afforded in the late Roald Dahl's autobiography of his schooldays, *Boy*. Dahl had the misfortune of being bullied by this woman some years earlier when he was a pupil at a school in Weston-super-Mare.

I stayed at this school for two years. I got on well with the boys and staff, with this one exception. I decided to leave after I had been shouted at for the umpteenth time because some wretched child had lost a glove – my fault obviously!

During my last term Sylvia and I drove to Norwich one weekend when I happened to be off duty. We called to see John Jevons who had been a master at Seaford during my time there and had gone on to be headmaster of a school in Norwich.

It was Jevons who told me of the exploits of Diarmaid Jennings, a pupil of Seaford College whom I knew well but, being slightly older than me, had left school a few terms earlier. He had always been mildly eccentric and after leaving school had gone on to take some training course where – Jevons told me – his behaviour had become even more amusingly off-beat. There was the occasion when Jennings had terrified his fellow students with a so-called poisonous spider which he knew to be harmless. Another time on a dark winter's night, Jennings, without betraying his presence, joined a search party who were, in fact, searching for him.

These two incidents struck me as good, humorous material and I used them, suitably altered, in the early series of my *Jennings At School* radio plays some years after the war. So it was to Jennings for his eccentricities and to Jevons for telling me about them that I owe a debt of gratitude for providing me with the germ of an idea that developed into a series of children's books and plays.

Finding a new job was not going to be easy. Most of those for which I could have applied were for bachelors prepared to live on the premises. But as a married man I could only take a non-resident post and hope to find rented accommodation that was within my means. Eventually I heard (from the almost legendary Gabbitas Thring) of a day prep-school in Brondesbury, London NW6. The headmaster had died and his son was needing someone to take it on with the proviso that the new headmaster was required to put up some capital to keep the school going. My mother most generously supplied me with the wherewithal to do this. It should have been a loan but World War Two seriously upset my plans and it was not until many years later that I was able to recompense her in any way.

The school, Vernon House, was a large Victorian building in Willesden Lane, built in the days when carriage drives (access and exit without having to turn the horses) were the order of the day. There was also an extension for dining rooms and classrooms, so there was plenty of room for the reduced number of pupils whom I found there upon my arrival. My first job was to try and increase the number of boys and my plans for this were going forward smoothly only to be thwarted one year later by the war.

It was here at Vernon House School in 1938 that my daughter Sally spent the first year of her life. She was born at Fretherne Nursing Home in Welwyn Garden City, where Sylvia had booked in for her confinement. In later life Sally married Ted, a schoolmaster, and in the course of time my grandchildren Tracy and Nicola were born. Both girls are now pursuing successful professional lives, Tracy as a business executive and Nicola as a dentist.

1938/39 was not an easy year to be embarking on a new venture. There was Munich with Neville Chamberlain assuring us of peace in our time; this didn't stop anyone preparing for war in our time and there was ceaseless activity about air raid precautions, civil defence, school evacuations and a general air of unrest and uncertainty about the future.

A fair number of the boys were Jewish so I had to familiarise myself with such things as the Jewish calendar for days when they would be absent for religious holidays. I also had to make provision for Hebrew lessons.

The school had a fair-sized rough playground, but no sports field. I had the playground tarmacked and I found a recreation ground where I could hire football pitches within walking distance. However a train journey was still necessary to get the boys to the swimming baths in Finchley Road.

I kept the staff who had been at the school with the previous headmaster. During the three terms of 1938/39, I increased the number of boys and – all in all – things were going reasonably well. But the threat of impending war, as 1939 rolled on, made life increasingly difficult. If or when war broke out, London schools would have to evacuate. Should I try to rent out some safe premises in the country? Not easy to do with rents rising and, more particularly, only a sketchy idea of what was involved. There were so many imponderables that I abandoned the idea of a private evacuation and signed up with the official council scheme to move the children of the cities into the country.

The crunch came in the summer holidays of 1939. By then many of the boys and their parents had dispersed of their own accord and could not be contacted. I was left with less than twenty evacuees, including a few girls from a neighbouring school, who joined up with us as they had no plans of their own.

Friday 1st September 1939 saw our orderly crocodile of evacuees, bearing suitcases and gasmasks, making their way to Willesden station behind our official banner, WN55. The platforms were crowded with contingents of children, most of whom were excited and apprehensive about this journey into the unknown that awaited them. The LCC's evacuation plans worked extremely well. Thousands of schoolchildren were transported into the country with the minimum of fuss. The problem came later; having got the kids out of the danger zone, what were they going to do with them next? Everything was in the lap of the gods. Trains came and went. Eventually we found our magic number WN55 on the window of a coach, which we duly boarded. We didn't know where we were going. The station staff didn't know where we were going. I can only guess that the engine driver had some inkling of our destination, but I can't be sure about this. After about an hour's journey, the train stopped and we were told to disembark. We were at Northampton; some of the school parties were marched off into the town to find accommodation. Others, including WN55, boarded a fleet of buses lined up in the station yard to be taken to villages in the countryside.

Our bus took us to Little Houghton, a small village straggling the Northampton-Bedford road. The whole village turned out to welcome (and gawp at) this invasion of foreigners from the outside world. Our party in ones and twos were adopted by local families and taken off to make themselves at home in their new environment. Sylvia, Sally (in pushchair) and I were claimed by a Mrs Bartlett, a friendly woman of some importance who lived in a large house in the village. There were, in point of fact, three large houses in Little Houghton. All the rest were cottages. There was a church, a butcher's shop and a general stores – and that's about all.

That evening, I did a round of the cottages to see how my school party was settling in and to make sure they had all sent postcards home to tell their parents where they were. Their hosts had gone out of their way to make them feel at home. They were being paid for it – just! The Government paid eight shillings and sixpence per week for each evacuee's bed and board.

The next morning, I, along with the oldest boys in the party, was taken back into Northampton and spent most of the day filling sandbags to protect the Town Hall. We returned to our billets tired and hungry.

War was declared next morning. Mrs Bartlett put her wireless set at our disposal so that we could listen to Chamberlain at 11 a.m. Though the announcement was of world-wide importance, our hostess had to miss it as it clashed with Matins at the church. I imagine that attendance at the service was minimal as the rest of the village was glued to its wireless sets.

It was a beautiful sunny day and we sat in the garden listening to the *wireless* (never called *radio* then) through the open drawing-room window. The Prime Minister's announcement was followed almost at once by the false alarm air raid sirens. This was disturbing as no one expected so immediate a reaction. But nothing happened and we were left wondering what sort of a war this was going to be. It was some months before we found out.

Lessons (if you can call them that) got going after the weekend in the vicarage dining room by kind permission of the Reverend J. Boodle. We had virtually no equipment or qualified staff, but the educated inhabitants of the village (and there were several) rallied round and provided some semblance of a volunteer force of teachers. Somehow we managed.

The most interesting facet of our sudden eruption upon the village community was sociological. A fair number of my boys were orthodox Jews. Without warning, they found themselves precipitated into a rural community with a different standard of values. The village children had never met any Jews before. The locals were of agricultural peasant stock; they had to get used to newcomers who wouldn't eat pork, ham or bacon; prayed with their caps on and didn't go to church. It took a bit of getting used to and sometimes led to embarrassing situations. I can remember an occasion when two Jewish parents came down to visit their son. Rationing was in force and as we felt obliged to feed them after their journey, we had *faute de mieux* to give them some sausages. They were too polite to refuse them but, after they had gone, we found the remains of the meal hidden amongst the ashes in the fireplace. I could see their point of view.

6

It soon became clear that something more permanent would have to be done to replace the haphazard schooling and accommodation that we were doing our best to cope with in the early days of September. The answer was to find suitable premises which could serve as a boarding school and so reconstitute our community as a proper educational establishment.

The vicar of Little Houghton had as part of his parish the neighbouring village of Brafield-on-the-Green (though we never found the *green*) about two miles further along the Bedford Road. The Parsonage at Brafield, a large rambling house adjoining the church, was occupied only by the vicar's curate; it was a residence impossibly vast for a single occupant. The curate was only too glad to seek comfortable lodgings in the village when I offered to rent the premises. The Parsonage had enough rooms for several classrooms and dormitories and a large garden, though the plumbing and ablution facilities left something to be desired. There was only one flush lavatory indoors, and another one in the large garden. There was only one bathroom (converted from a bedroom) so washing and bathing would have to be regulated on a very strict timetable.

I decided to rent The Parsonage and we moved in during November. At this time we had only a few boarders as some of the original party had gone home, as things were quiet; they came back again when the raids started. I arranged for a furniture van to bring down desks and school equipment from Willesden Lane. As those premises had been left empty since September, they had been burgled and vandalised in common with most other vacant property in London. I had to go up to Willesden Lane quite frequently to see what was going on and when I reported to the police that nearly all the lead pipes had been wrenched out of the walls and stolen, they took me to a large warehouse which was crammed from floor to ceiling with stolen pipes which they had recovered. They then asked me if I could identify my property. Difficult! One length of pipe looks to me very like any other length of pipe.

During the weeks that followed, we became a sustainable community. Our housekeeper from Brondesbury and our two domestics joined us. The latter were lads from up North, who had been trained as house-men by the Scout movement in a bid to relieve the chronic unemployment on Tyneside. We didn't have them for long as they were soon called up for military service. However, we had no shortage of helpers.

I was extremely fortunate in finding two young women teachers, who lived in a neighbouring village. These were sisters, Barbara and Kathleen Lines, who stayed with the school throughout the war. When the war finished and I joined up my remaining boys with St Lawrence College, Barbara joined too – and married the headmaster! We were joined by other teachers who came and went. Some were good, others, so-so; ranging from excellent at the top to odd-balls and nutcases lower down.

The Brafield locals soon got used to us and helped us in many different ways. There was a farmyard abutting our garden wall and another a short distance away, which provided us with milk. We bought some hens and two pigs, all of which helped out with our rations. One of the farmers allowed us to use a providentially flat field as a football pitch; a neighbour made us a splendid pair of goal posts and in no time at all we were challenging the local village school to a match – which they won!

So we were managing fairly well, all things considered – apart from the plumbing! The trouble was that the village water supply came from a water tank, which was roughly on the level with our first floor bathroom. When the tank was full we had no problem, but when the water level dropped, the bathroom tank had to be filled by my running up and down the steep back stairs twenty-five times, carrying two-gallon buckets up from the kitchen.

With only one indoor lavatory, there was always a cross-legged queue outside the door, clamouring for admission. This wasn't made easier on the occasion that David, a disturbed little boy, locked himself in and threw the key out of the window into a patch of nettles below. By the time we had retrieved the key, the queue was performing a dervish dance of which St Vitus would have been proud.

I registered for military service with the nation's 27-year-olds. The medical examination was somewhat perfunctory. Having proved that I could see, hear, stand on one leg and wasn't suffering from beri-beri, flat-footedness or hernia, I passed my medical with flying colours. (Perhaps the flying colours showed that I wasn't colour blind either.) There was always a delay of several months between the registration and the call-up, during which time one was expected to enrol in some sort of national service in addition to the day job. This was the *Dad's Army* syndrome, though by the time that television got to grips with the comic potentialities of the situation, the TV series should rightly have been entitled *Grandad's Army*. I joined the Auxiliary Fire Service as my friend, Bob Clayton, who had joined up in London, suggested that this was a more interesting way of spending the time than marching up and down shouldering a broom handle in place of a rifle. All this meant that I could continue to run the school in the day time, but on several nights of the week I reported for fire service drill in the evenings and spent the night at a fire station in Northampton, ready to turn out with a fire crew if duty called.

The phoney war was over by this time and by the way things were going I reckoned that I would be called up for the army at any time in the summer of 1940. But then Dunkirk happened and shortly afterwards the Luftwaffe started their bombing raids on London. The result was that the army authorities were overwhelmed by the number of troops, English and Allied, who had so suddenly been repatriated and couldn't be used in a military capacity because at the time everything was in a state of flux.

There were just too many soldiers standing around with nothing to do. On the other hand, there was a shortage of firemen now that the raids had started. Overnight, I became a full-time member of the AFS, shortly to be reconstituted as the National Fire Service.

So, there was now no one to take charge of the school full time, though I was able to get home when I was off duty. I appointed a headmaster who was reasonably efficient, but not all that likeable. Eventually he went, and I replaced him with one who was very grand but not much good at the job. He taught the senior boys to play bridge, but that was about the extent of his headmastership.

Northampton was never the target of the Luftwaffe attacks, which in our area were concentrated on Birmingham, Coventry, Leicester and Nottingham. We were called out to help deal with these raids, but returned to our home base when we were no longer needed. I missed the great Coventry Blitz as I was on leave on the night and the only time I went on an important regional call was to the Liverpool docks in 1941. The night journey to Liverpool was the coldest I can ever remember; we were in the back of an open lorry in sub-zero temperatures. We stopped for a few minutes at Chesterfield at 3am and the cup of tea I was given was the most welcome cup of tea I can remember drinking. We were in Liverpool for the best part of a week. We went to various fires in different parts of the docks but, not knowing the city, I had no clear idea of our whereabouts. We were stationed in a large building with a glass roof. When called out to a job, we followed a motorbike dispatch rider to wherever we were summoned.

In these early days I was allotted to a substation near the town centre where we had to mount a guard at the entrance all through the night. One night, or rather in the early hours of the morning, one of our aircraft, returning from a mission, made a forced landing in a street near the town centre. The fireman on guard duty, without waiting for instructions, left his post and ran to the aid of the stricken aircraft. Moments later, the bells "went down" for the night crew to turn out on an appliance – which they did, all except one member of the crew, who was too late to leap aboard before the tender started off. Not to be outdone, the laggard pursued the rapidly receding fire engine on foot. The effect was farcical; a turn-out to a crashed aircraft consisting of, in the lead, one fireman on foot, followed by a crew on a tender, followed in turn by another fireman on foot running along behind. Fortunately there were no serious casualties, though the aircraft was a "write-off" as one might expect.

For some while, I was on a crew at this substation; there was always a shortage of drivers and, as I was the owner of a modest Morris Minor, it was assumed that I was qualified to drive any fire-engine, or, indeed, any vehicle or appliance that needed to be driven, without any further practice or instruction. This I managed to do without giving away the fact that I frequently found myself in the driving seat of a vehicle about which I knew very little: for example, how many gears has it got? How do I find reverse without an inconvenient collision? The old red engines had the gear lever and the brake outside on the running board so you had to lean perilously outside the vehicle to change gear and there was a loud grinding of gears if you failed to double-declutch smartly.

I was on leave on Christmas Day 1942 and had taken the family to Welwyn Garden City to see my mother. Christmas Day at the fire station was celebrated with an extra special dinner at midday. My crew had just sat down at the canteen table when the bells "went down" and they were sent on a fire call to – of all places – Vernon House School at Brafield. It so happened that I had let some rooms in the building to Alex Reeve, the director of the Northampton Rep. He had allowed the stove to overheat and start a small fire. By the time my crew had returned from coping with the outbreak of a small fire, their beautiful Christmas dinner had congealed into an inedible concoction of seasonal fare. When I reported for duty on Boxing Day I was hardly the flavour of the month. No, I had not devised a devilish scheme to ruin their Christmas, I protested vehemently.

A few months later, I was summoned for an interview at Nottingham, which was the area fire headquarters. I was offered the rank of Station Officer, which was certainly a good promotion, but involved being transferred to a different area in East Anglia, and it became clear it was an administrative desk job. This I didn't want and, though I had no right to refuse, I managed to avoid the transfer by explaining that I wanted to continue as an operational fireman rather than spend twelve hours every day glued to a desk. This was probably a black mark on my record, but it didn't seem to matter as quite soon afterwards I was promoted to Leading Fireman. This I enjoyed as I now had my own crew; they were a great bunch of lads, some of whom stayed on my crew until the course of the war changed with the Allied invasion of Europe and everything was again in a state of flux.

Until then, there were weeks of comparative inactivity on the home front (apart from the V1 and V2 buzz bomb attacks) but we were too far inland to be in the firing line. I do however remember seeing a buzz bomb which suddenly shot over the garden at Brafield when I was at home and off duty. I was upstairs in a bedroom with Sally (aged about four or five). I pushed her under the bed until the bomb had passed overhead. We awaited the crunch, which we heard some moments later when the bomb exploded about six miles away. These buzz bombs engendered an understandable, but morally dubious, reaction in the population of Southern England. As people heard the approach of the flying bomb, the universal prayer was "keep going, let it keep going!" – the origin perhaps of "not in my back yard."

During these fairly long spells of comparative inactivity – apart from attending chimney fires and haystacks ablaze on various farms – I was able to take part in the Fire Service drama productions and also act with the Northampton Drama Club. At about this time I wrote my first full length play. It was called *Industrial Front* and was about factory workers in wartime. There was also a fireman (naturally!) and a Russian engineer who had been sent to England to advise on a technical problem connected with RAF bomber engines. I couldn't get it produced professionally, but we agreed to make it a Fire Service production. It was typed, cast, and just about to go into rehearsal when the invasion of Europe started. Some fire service personnel were sent down to the South Coast to cope with whatever might happen during our invasion; my cast disappeared overnight and the production was naturally cancelled. So ended *Industrial Front*; it was never produced, but I still think it was a well-made play.

Tim was born in 1941, when Sally was three, and though we managed to feed them well, rationing was strict, so in their early years they had to manage with a meagre sweet ration. Their first taste of an ice-cream was not until the war was over and I remember Sally being puzzled when she was given her first banana. How did one eat these new-fangled fruits? ("No, dear, you have to peel it; banana skins are not edible.")

As the end of the war was approaching I had to give some thought to the future. It would not have been easy to restart the school in London. The premises had been taken over as Council offices, so I could not get the lease renewed, and in any case my original boys had grown up and my connection with the parents had become remote. It would mean starting from scratch with no money and no facilities. The boys I had at Brafield would soon be passing on to the next stage of their education and there was none to follow after. St Lawrence College of Ramsgate had evacuated to Courteenhall, a village a few miles from Northampton where they had taken over, for the duration, a country mansion owned by Sir Hereward Wake, a genial bluff aristocrat who traced his family back to the historical Hereward the Wake. He was so typical of the traditional stereotype of the landed gentry that I used him as a model for my character Sir Ichabod Moulting when later I came to write the plays and the book *A Funny Thing Happened* in 1953.

During the earlier war years, I had sent several boys to St Lawrence College. Now I sent the rest of my boarders to join them and joined their staff myself at the beginning of the summer term 1945. I was sorry to say goodbye to my fire crew – Charlie, Bert Race and others. I never saw them again, though I exchanged Christmas letters with Bert until he died in 1996.

St Lawrence College comprised the junior (IAPS) prep school and the senior school. At Ramsgate, the two schools occupied separate buildings and separate, but adjoining, sports fields. The junior and senior boys were not allowed to enter each other's territory. At Courteenhall, such rigid isolation was not possible. After the summer term, 1945, the junior school moved back to Ramsgate and the seniors returned for the following Easter term.

I was appointed as senior master under the headmaster W.G. Waymouth. I wasn't really senior to any other masters for at this time with permanent staff still away in the forces most of the teachers were women. In any case, my seniority was temporary; Keith Roberts, then an army major, had been senior master before the war and it was only fair that he should have his old job back on his return. Waymouth was a good disciplinarian; too good really, as his coldly dignified approach to life in general meant that all the boys were cowed into silence whenever he made an appearance. It was sad to see a room full of boys, happily engaged in playing games or chatting animatedly, come to a sudden silent stop as W.G.W. appeared in the doorway.

7

In August 1945, we packed up all our possessions, sold the desks and school equipment and made tracks for Ramsgate. We rented a flat owned by the Council overlooking the harbour with wonderful views of the shipping; on a clear day we could see Calais. It was a busy prospect of boats and day-trippers who thronged the seaside town in large numbers. With the war over, everyone seemed to be spending a holiday on the Thanet coast. From our window we looked down at the whelk stalls (I tried one saucer of whelks, but that was more than enough), the "genuine" Newmarket Jockey scales ("I guess your weight or money back"), religious missions on the beach ("What a Friend we have in Jesus!"), and fortune-tellers in their tiny tents ("Madame X, from the mysterious East"). Well, Ramsgate is almost East, isn't it! Motorboat trips to the Cork lightship and the Goodwin Sands. The whole world was below our front window.

Sally and Tim went to school at the convent. Sally had previously been at Northampton High School, a bus ride from Brafield, but it was Tim's first entry into school life. It was a good school, though the building seemed a bit overcrowded with large statues of the Blessed Virgin Mary on the landings.

When Sally and Tim were old enough, Sally went to Clarendon House, the local grammar school, where she did well and, having decided that PE was her choice for the future, she was accepted for Chelsea College of PE at Eastbourne, where she qualified for the teaching profession. Tim went first to St Lawrence Junior School and then on to the College. He wanted to be a farmer; he spent a year at Cirencester and finished his qualifications at Dorchester Agricultural Institute... But all that was in the future.

From 1946 to 1952 our home was the Ramsgate flat. I cycled each day to the junior school where I was in charge of English teaching and, despite some opposition, I managed to include

Drama as a class subject and staged some school productions. The opposition stemmed from the fact that St Lawrence was evangelical in its outlook and just didn't approve of plays (especially if they were well acted!); it was all very well to mock drama by burlesque and bad acting, but to take drama seriously was something that simply was not done. Indeed, the Great Hall at the College had been donated by a wealthy politician, and it was understood that it should not be used for theatrical performances. So that was one thing that needed changing and I managed to achieve this thanks to the more progressive ideas of the staff returning after World War Two. I was therefore able to produce a junior school play every summer and this became a very popular event.

There was in Ramsgate a professional theatre of weekly repertory productions staged in an enormous theatre built in the 1890s by "Lord" George Sanger, a circus impresario. The company at the Palace Theatre consisted of about ten actors/actresses including the producer, stage management, *et al.* During the holidays and sometimes during the term, I was recruited to the cast and acted with them in about twenty productions.

Weekly repertory is, or was – as it doesn't seem to exist any more – one of the most exhausting and nerve-battering ways of earning a living that I can call to mind. The actor has two full-length plays occupying his brain at the same time, i.e. the play he is currently performing, the play he is rehearsing for next week, while also trying to forget the play he performed the week before. All this has to be done on six rehearsals. The schedule for a 3-act play went like this:

Monday – dress rehearsal for the week's offering with curtain-up for first performance at 7.30pm.

Tuesday – Morning: read through plus stage directions of next week's play. Afternoon: learn the whole of Act 1. Evening: 7.30pm curtain-up for second performance of this week's offering.

Wednesday – Morning: rehearse Act 1 without books. Afternoon: learn Act 2. Evening: 7.30pm third performance of current production.

Thursday – Act 2 without books. Learn Act 3 – perform in evening.

Friday – Act 3 followed by Acts 1 and 2. Perform in evening.

Saturday – Morning: whole play rehearsal. Afternoon: Matinee followed by evening performance

Sunday – In theory, no rehearsals – free all day, but don't count on it! There were always bits which had to be seen to.

And so, on to Monday dress rehearsal, plus first performance, and the weekly cycle starts all over again.

With so little free time for study, when did the rep actor learn his or her lines? Some with big parts stayed up half the night and few were word perfect for the first night. Technique was the thing that helped them through and, provided that the cues didn't go astray, the audience was not fully aware that the author's lines were approximately, but not literally, being spoken. One or two of the company seemed to learn their parts without difficulty. Alec Mason, who ran the company, had an almost photographic memory and could learn virtually the whole play after reading it a few times; others suffered agonies and sleepless nights. I came somewhere between these extremes. I never needed assistance from the prompter but, unlike Alec, I had to work hard. The oldest member of the company had such trouble in learning his lines that he was almost pathetically grateful to be cast as the character with the least to say.

One evening, when we were performing *Outward Bound*, his memory just packed up; but he wouldn't stop talking. There were two other actors besides me on stage and we kept trying to break in; we could have got the dialogue flowing again if only he had let us, but he just kept on talking. Somehow or other we managed to finish the scene. When afterwards we asked him why he wouldn't let us in, he said "I felt that if I stopped talking, I could never start again."

Things like that happened with so few rehearsals. On another occasion, I was on stage when an actress missed an entrance. For a time we improvised with artificial dialogue about the weather and offering each other whisky from the drinks cabinet, which proved to be empty when I opened the door. "Oh dear! The butler's forgotten to replenish the Scotch." I could see the ASM in the wings and made faces at him indicating our plight. But he thought I was being funny and made rabbits' ears back at me. At last the penny dropped and he rushed off to fetch the absent actress. When at last she made an entrance, she was in the wrong clothes. She had forgotten that she had another entrance in Act 2 and had changed into a nightdress – her costume for Act 3. Another time, there was an unfortunate contretemps. A cue in Act 1 was very similar to a cue in Act 3. An actor, who had been fed the Act 1 cue, replied with the line from Act 3. This was taken up and ten minutes after the rise, the cast found themselves heading towards the final curtain. Somehow, again, a crisis was averted. But what a way to earn a living!

The only time I had a bad fright was in a Christmas production of *Treasure Island.* In Act 1, I played Blind Pew who gets killed at the end of the Act, enabling me to play Ben Gunn, the castaway, for the rest of the play. Ben Gunn, having been on the island for some years, had a beard that came down to his chest. It was hot and, when I came off stage after Ben's first appearance, I tossed the vital property aside in the dressing room. As the time approached for my next entrance, I made ready for my cue only to find that the beard had disappeared. This was incredible. It was only a small dressing room and there was nowhere that the beard could be concealed. The entrance cue was rapidly drawing near. What was to be done? Having made my exit with a foot long bush attached to my chin, the audience could hardly be persuaded that a clean-shaven Ben Gunn had borrowed a razor from one of the ship's company. At the last moment, I found it. I had tossed the horrible article into my make-up box and, unobserved by me, the lid had fallen down with the beard inside. So the hirsute castaway was able to make his entrance with a split second to spare.

Alec, our director, had understudied Laurence Olivier in Congreve's *Love for Love* in London, and decided to produce it with the Palace Players. But the play was long, too long to be filled into a matinee with the evening performance at 7.30pm. So, after the Friday performance, we gathered on stage while Alec dictated enormous cuts, some of several pages, which was to be the script for the Saturday matinee before returning to the full length version for the second house on Saturday night. It was a murderous ordeal, trying to remember where the cuts came, with cues altered and pages deleted. I doubt whether the matinee ever went according to plan – but it went, and everything was back to normal – or vaguely back to normal – for the evening performance.

I wrote a play for the rep at about this time; it was called *Draw The Line Somewhere* and concerned a family turning up for a holiday at a rented house, only to find it double-booked to some very devious characters. It was quite a success; the audience loved it and I tried to get it accepted by a London management, but it didn't get anywhere. The trouble was it was too topical, involving a US Army deserter on the run, and various ploys about food shortages, ration books and the black market. It would have been dated after a few months, so it never got anywhere near the West End; but I enjoyed writing it – and acting in it, too.

It could be dangerous playing at the Palace. We put on a fairly ridiculous farce wherein it fell to my lot to take refuge in a shed where dynamite had been stored. The scene ended with an explosion inside the hut, which promptly collapsed as I came running out with most of my clothes blown off by the blast. For the explosion, the stage manager had got hold of some maroons from the local Lifeboat station. One of these placed in a dustbin in the hut was detonated by remote control from the lighting box. The control wasn't nearly remote enough for me, a few feet from the dustbin crouching down with my fingers stuck in my ears. It worked brilliantly, though I was somewhat deaf for the rest of the performance and lucky to escape being seriously hurt. There was never an inspection by the safety authority at the rep. I stopped playing with the rep when they moved to another theatre and eventually disintegrated.

There was another company at Broadstairs who contacted me on one occasion. One afternoon, I received a telegram (we had no phone in those days) asking me to come at once as they'd had an emergency; an actor had a row with the producer and walked out after the first night. I agreed to help out to the best of my ability – such as it was. I didn't know the play, *Love from a Stranger*, but it was a very small part, and on my first performance I managed to get by with the script concealed in my hat (carried, not worn!). The real trouble was that there was no time for rehearsal and I had never met any members of the company before. Neither did I know which parts they were playing. Thus, when I arrived on stage, I didn't know to which member of the cast I was supposed to be speaking. It was better for the rest of the week when I had learned my words. They asked me to play the following week, but I decided that I had had enough!

I was enjoying my job at St Lawrence, teaching English and supervising football and cricket and taking a stint of supervision duty every week; in what free time was left I began writing radio plays. These were fairly run-of-the-mill efforts for programmes called *Wednesday Matinee* and *Saturday Matinee*. In those days, the author would send a play to the BBC drama department, and within a very short space of time would get a reply and know whether or not his work was accepted. I was lucky; mine were accepted. Today it is very different. You first have to contact a (usually anonymous) commissioning editor and submit endless synopses, sample dialogue, sample extension of development etc.

etc. Then, although they haven't read the play, they frequently tell you that there is no slot for your efforts.

I can't think how the young writer of today ever manages to break into radio writing. We used to say that what mattered was luck plus ability. Today, you still need the ability but luck plus "whom you know" has become the more important element coupled, perhaps, with the vital importance of being in the right place at the right time.

I had no intention of ever becoming a writer for children, but I think it was probably the fact of being on dormitory duty that provided the germ of the idea behind the *Jennings* stories. It would start with a bribe: "If you're all in bed in 30 seconds I'll tell you a story." It always worked.

Having exhausted my scant repertoire of other people's stories, I had to start making them up myself. There had to be a hero, and gradually the plots centred round one particular character. I remembered Diarmaid Jennings, whose exploits served as a starting point. After this source material was used up, I had to invent more stories and introduced further characters into the plots. They were not based upon particular individuals, but were an amalgam of various people I had met. Thus, although I had known boys like Darbishire and masters like Mr Wilkins, they were only the skeketons of my *dramatis personae* and had to be fleshed out to become the final characters that I had in mind.

I have always preferred writing comedy and whatever the situation I have usually chosen to dwell on the lighter side of events; and merely by keeping my eyes and ears open as I walked round the school and noted what was happening, I gathered a store of material which I could shape to suit the personality of my characters. Much of the comedy came from noting the different way in which a situation would be viewed from the adult and the youthful point of view. For example, boys will explode with hilarity at some fatuous joke which leaves Mr Wilkins baffled. However, the reader can often be amused by the reaction of the characters to something that he, the reader, doesn't think is funny at all.

The first Jennings play which I wrote in 1948 was meant as a "one-off." I had no intention of writing a sequel – let alone a series – when I sent the script to BBC Drama. They passed it on to *Children's Hour* whereupon David Davis wrote asking me to come and see him. This I did. I walked into his office and tripped over a stack of gramophone records just inside the door, scattering them across the room. Not a good first entrance to Broadcasting House, but all was well. David and all the *Children's Hour* department liked the play and wanted me to write a series of six. The first *Jennings at School* was broadcast in October 1948 and was the forerunner of a series which went on until 1964, when *Children's Hour* was killed by the "death of a thousand cuts" and vanished into thin air.

Children's Hour held a competition twice a year. It was called *Request Week* and listeners voted for a repeat of their favourite programmes. *Jennings* managed to come top each time, so although I wrote only sixty-two separate plays about Jennings there were many more than a hundred transmissions.

David made an excellent choice for the main adult characters and chose Geoffrey Wincott to play Mr Carter and Wilfred Babbage as Mr Wilkins. These two played in every script and became very popular with the listeners in their contrasting roles. The boys, of course, had to be changed when their voices broke and they sounded too old for their parts. Having outgrown Jennings, several of them went on to make a new reputation in the media as adults.

The cast started to rehearse on the afternoon before transmission and continued on the morning and afternoon of the following day until it was time for the broadcast. In the early days, transmissions were "live," though later on everything was recorded. "Live" transmission meant that if anything went wrong "on air," the fluff was heard by everyone listening. David was very strict with the boys about audible page-turning and anything that could affect the performance. Once, during a broadcast, all was going well until a boy playing Atkinson turned over two pages of his script at the same time. He didn't at first realise what he had done, and disaster was looming as the dialogue became gobbledegook. Fortunately, Geoffrey Wincott was also at the microphone and by some quick thinking managed to *ad lib* for some moments until the boy had found the right place. But it was awkward while it lasted.

David's tight hold on the cast never relaxed. I was in the control room watching a *Jennings* rehearsal when the script, as a result of some supposedly horrific situation, called for some lively *ad-libbing*. Amidst cries of "Gosh! Wow! Help," etc. one boy said "Damn!" David stopped the rehearsal at once and said to the culprit, "If you say that again, you'll be out in the street – and so shall I." The ghost of Lord Reith nodded approvingly.

Fortunately for me, the end of *Children's Hour* was not the end of *Jennings* on radio. A few years later, children's programmes were restarted in a programme called *Fourth Dimension* which ran from 1970 to 1974. David Davis had retired and the *Jennings* plays were produced by Herbert Smith in Manchester. Wilfred Babbage was not available and I played Mr Wilkins, a part I very much enjoyed.

I also wrote a serial for *Children's Hour* called *A Funny Thing Happened*. As its name implies, it was a comedy but Derek McCullogh (Uncle Mac) produced it and I didn't think his production was funny at all. More like Ibsen in one of his gloomy moods. But Mac retired soon afterwards and David gave it a second production. This time it really sounded as though a funny thing *had* happened. A few years later, it had yet another good production with yet another producer – a rare event in *Children's Hour* programmes. *A Funny Thing Happened* was published as a book in 1953. The advantage of being an actor as well as a writer is that you can usually pull rank to get yourself cast in your own plays. This happened again when I was asked at short notice to write a serial for BBC Radio. I obliged with *Liz*, a six-part comedy with a cast of mainly teenage girls. I played Collins, the caretaker of a block of London flats – a very different character from Mr Wilkins.

With *Jennings at School* firmly established on radio, I decided to re-tell the stories in narrative form. A book is a very different kettle of fish from a radio play and although I made use of some of the same incidents I obviously had to take the material to pieces and rework it as a book. The first title, *Jennings Goes to School*, was published in 1950 and still sits on the bookshop shelves alongside *That's Jennings,* published in 1994. And in between there is the rest of the series of 25 titles which have been on sale for nearly half a century.

Jennings Goes to School was accepted by William Collins (no Harper in those days) and I was offered the usual contract prevailing at that time. In the 1940s, most children's fiction was bought outright and few authors received a royalty of any sort. I was offered £150 for the copyright and, knowing no better, I accepted it as they told me it was the rate for the job. The book was published and sold very well, helped by the free publicity from BBC *Children's Hour* where the plays had become well-established. And that, I thought, was the end of the matter so far as the contract was concerned. However, I became friendly with one of Collins' reps, William Hartstone, who took me with him on his tour of the bookshops in his area and arranged for me to give talks to schools and libraries. He was impressed by the way in which the book was selling and realised its potential for a best-selling series of future titles. Unknown to me, he approached the Collins editorial board and said, in effect, "You are not being fair to Buckeridge, fobbing him off with an outright payment. You should give him a royalty." Which they did!

This first book has, over the years, sold thousands of copies in English and in translation into a dozen languages; it is still selling fifty years later. Under the original agreement, I should not have earned a penny in royalties over the last fifty years. I am eternally grateful to Bill Hartstone for persuading Collins to tear up the original "all rights" contract and replace it with something a lot more encouraging to a would-be author.

So now I was ready to start work on more *Jennings* books which, with my other writing, were to keep me busy for more than forty years. I planned each book out in detail before starting work, although I soon found out that the plan could legitimately be altered if the characters or the situation appeared to be heading in a different direction from the one I had first envisaged.

Normally, my plan was to take a genuine situation that the readers could identify with, something quite ordinary and unremarkable that was happening as part of the normal routine of school. Having done that, I would allow the situation to develop one step further than it would have been allowed to develop in real life. Boys are imaginative and are continually planning wonderful and improbable schemes and adventures, which sound brilliant in theory, but come to nothing when they are nipped in the bud by a master who sees that things threaten to get out of hand. But if the zeal of the masters can be logically delayed or diverted in some way for just long enough to enable the wonderful scheme to proceed a little further than it would have been allowed to go in real life, you are creating a situation which can lead to an entertaining climax.

Much of the comedy in *Jennings Goes To School* and its successors depends upon the contrasting way in which a situation can be interpreted by the adult as opposed to the youthful point of view. Boys will say things and do things which to them are perfectly logical, but appear incomprehensible to an adult who lacks the facility of looking into the developing mind and interpreting what is going on there. There is enough comic material to be found in this aspect of the youthful/adult character to fill more books than I shall ever write.

I have been lucky in the fact that Collins, my original publishers (the books are now published by Macmillan) sold the translation rights of my first and subsequent books to so many different countries. Though delighted, I am puzzled by this. Why should a book set in the milieu of an English prep school be so popular with foreign readers to whom boarding schools are almost unknown and school uniforms must appear as some sort of fancy dress? What, for example, do the Norwegians or the Indonesians or the Chinese make of eleven-year-old English schoolboys playing cricket...? I sometimes wonder!

8

In 1950, I had to make a decision. I had a full-time teaching job at St Lawrence and enough writing with books and plays to keep me fully occupied. I had, in short, two jobs and would soon be unable to do justice to both of them. I decided to give up teaching and become a writer. I resigned from St Lawrence, hoping for the best.

We were still living in Ramsgate when the first three Jennings books were published, and the flat overlooking the harbour was too small to allow any space for full-time writing. I looked round for an office to rent and found a top-floor turret room over the pub next door to the Palace Theatre. The turret was circular so instead of pacing up and down in search of inspiration I just walked round and round in circles. It was a new and daunting experience to face the fact that I had burned my boats and I was on my own so far as making a living was concerned. I needed to branch out and add a few more activities to my workload. We also needed more living space; with Sally and Tim growing rapidly, the flat was bursting at the seams.

I had heard about the Reverend Marcus Morris who, aghast at the craze for horror comics imported from the USA, decided to publish a wholesome type of weekly "comic" paper in an effort to stem the flow of unsuitable reading for the young. His weekly paper was called *Eagle* and immediately became very successful and enjoyed a large circulation for some years. The main character was Dan Dare, who enjoyed all sorts of exciting adventures in and around his space ship. Virtually the whole of the comic was in strip cartoon and I felt that what was lacking was a good read. I went to see Marcus Morris and agreed to write a series of stories for the paper, featuring the adventures of a group of boys at a London day school. The result was *Rex Milligan* who became very popular and whose misadventures appeared in weekly "one-off" stories. I still think that *Rex Milligan* was just as good and just as funny as Jennings; but despite four full-length books and a BBC TV series, he never became as popular as Jennings and his cronies.

Eventually, we moved to Sandwich (in 1952); a fascinating little town with a history going back to Norman times. Indeed, its medievalism is still evident wherever you look. For instance, the streets of Sandwich are never quite straight, which gives you more hope of avoiding an arrow in your back or, at any rate, frustrating your enemies' chance of a direct hit.

Old traditions never die in Sandwich; the curfew was rung every night at eight o'clock from the belfry in St Peter's church. (Tim, when a teenager, was on the rota of ringers.) The Mayor of Sandwich wears a black gown, unlike the Mayors of the Cinque Ports, who wear scarlet robes. This is because the town, or at any rate the Mayor, is still in mourning for the citizens killed or raped by the rascally French when they raided the town in the thirteenth century. The Mayor also carries a slender bough of hazelwood on formal occasions. This is to ward off any witches who may be in the vicinity. Some of the street names are quaint; Holy Ghost Alley is one of my favourites. Our address was 2 The Ramparts which, with a little imagination, could be made to sound like Henry V urging his troops into the attack – especially as 2 The Ramparts was situated in Knightrider Street.

Most of our garden was at the front of the house; from our gate you crossed Knightrider Street, a cul-de-sac, and entered St Clement's churchyard with gravestones dating back hundreds of years. Some of the names on the headstones were followed by the inscription "AN IVRAT OF THE TOWN." At first, I couldn't think what an IVRAT could be until I worked out that IV was the Latin equivalent of what we should now write as JU. The jurats were obviously worthy forefathers of the town.

Gran, an unassuming and generous person, sold her house at Ferring to buy the Sandwich house, which she made over to me for the family. Sally and Tim went to school by bus and later Tim made the journey on his Lambretta, which was the pride of his teenage years. He had daydreams of travelling the world on his Lambretta. This never happened! But he did set out with his school friend, John Reed, to tour various countries of Europe. This lasted until the Lambretta broke down miles from home, and they had to return by public transport.

The Barbican Players was an amateur group, which I joined and acted with for ten years. It was a small group and during the 1950s the plays were staged in a typical church hall – typical because it had virtually no backstage area and no wing space. If your part called for you to exit left and make your next appearance Stage Right, you had to leave the building by a side door, and walk (sometimes run) out into the street and travel round the exterior of the building to arrive at the door on the opposite side. After some years of St Peter's Hall, we searched for more suitable premises and found an unoccupied building owned by Hovis McDougall, the bakery chain. We spent a lot of energy and a small amount of money in turning the place into a little theatre. The first full-length play we put on there was Ustinov's *Romanov and Juliet*. Looking back, I doubt whether all our effort was worth it for, although the project was great fun, the Town Council a few years later provided the Barbican Players with even better facilities at the town's Guildhall. This, of course, they could well afford to do because Sandwich was a very rich little town. Much of the wealth came from receipts from the toll bridge on the River Stour over which all vehicles had to pass when entering or leaving Thanet. There was no way of avoiding the bridge without a detour of about twenty miles to a crossing called Plucks Gutter, an intriguing name, but a time-consuming journey.

Sandwich had obtained its right to own a toll bridge at some medieval date and with a charge of a shilling to the driver of every vehicle coming or going from 6am till midnight it is no wonder that Sandwich was the envy of nearby towns like Dover or Deal. Whereas these neighbouring towns deplored traffic congestion in their streets, Sandwich could afford to have a tolerant view of all these motorists queuing up to fill the municipal coffers to overflowing. Now, alas, Sandwich has lost its right to coin money, but it was certainly lucrative while it lasted. Oh, my, how the money rolled in!

I was still writing a new *Jennings* book every year plus radio plays and stories for magazines. The books were becoming best-sellers and were selling 70,000 copies a year. This figure was increasing and by the mid-fifties it topped 100,000 – all in hardback. The best result was in 1957 when the sales reached 117,000. At the same time, Collins was negotiating foreign rights. *Jennings* appeared in French, German, Norwegian, Swedish, Danish, Hebrew, Spanish, Portuguese, Finnish, Indonesian, Dutch and most recently Chinese. Some of these fell by the wayside after one edition had been sold out, but others went on for some years. At the moment, the French and Norwegian sales are keeping up well and both sell more copies than the regular English editions in the UK. I find this surprising, particularly in the case of Norway with a population of only about three million. A lot of this must be due to my translator Nils Reinhardt Christensen. Nils was not only a translator of the books and radio plays (still going on Norsk Rikskring kasting) but a film producer/director as well. In Norway, Jennings is called Stompa (and in France, Bennet; in German editions he is called Fredy). Nils made three full-length films about Stompa, which went well in Scandinavia but didn't materialise elsewhere. I was very fond of Nils and his wife Siri and visited them many times but, sadly, Nils died a few years ago.

Collins' children's books were published by two separate departments. The more expensive books were published in London and the cheaper editions, which included the *Jennings* titles, were issued from Glasgow. I suggested that Jennings might well be switched to the up-market London department, but Charles Evans, the sales director, disagreed. He said that this might result in selling a few dozen more copies to Harrods or Hatchards, but we should lose our very flourishing market in what he described as "the back streets of West Hartlepool." Charles won the argument; Jennings stayed with Glasgow.

Sidney Goldsack was a Collins director, who joined the firm as a rep when Sir William (Billy) Collins was Chairman. I was told that on Sidney's first day as a salesman, touring the bookshops for orders, it was announced that all the reps must report back to the boardroom for a meeting called by the Chairman for 6.30pm.

When the appointed hour struck, all the staff were present except Sidney. This was hardly the way to impress Sir William with your devotion to duty, especially on your first day in a new job and, when eventually Sidney arrived, he was taken to task by the Chairman who demanded to know why he was late. Sidney explained; he was late because he had just sold a quarter of a million copies of the Bible, an amount so stupendous and unheard-of that jaws dropped all round the boardroom table. Sir Billy couldn't believe his ears. In one day Sidney had sold more Bibles than the firm reckoned to sell in ten years. How had this happened? Sidney explained; he had got to hear that the head of an American evangelical missionary society was in London replenishing the society's stock. Goldsack traced him to his hotel, called on him and proposed a deal on advantageous terms. Sidney apologised for being a few minutes late!

In the Ramsgate days, we usually spent a good deal of the summer holidays at Ferring but, after the move to Sandwich, we began taking our holidays abroad. We bought a second-hand Morris Minor with an open top and headed through France towards the Med. Four bodies in a small car was all very well for travelling, but not well at all when we couldn't get beds and had to spend the night in a semi-recumbent position in the sardine tin discomfort of the Morris. It was this problem of accommodation in the holiday season in France that suggested camping as a better bet than hotels with no vacancies. So I bought a Dormobile, an early model as the vogue for camping vans was only just starting.

During the next few years, we spent holidays in France, usually on the Mediterranean, once on the Western coast and finally in Denmark. The camping van solved a lot of accommodation problems, but it was always a bit of a squash.

The camping van proved useful in a different direction in 1961. The family were loyal members of CND and when we heard about the march from Aldermaston to London, we decided to give it our support over the four day Easter march. Sally was away for Easter, but Sylvia, Tim and I drove up for the Good Friday start. Tim marched all the way and I drove the Dormobile, which quite unofficially got taken over as a band wagon. The band (chiefly brass, I seem to remember) would play the marchers off at each stage and we could then overtake them and drive on to welcome them at the next official stopping point. The van suffered a bit with musicians and instruments squashed in like sardines, but it survived. The atmosphere on the march was positive and earnest. Canon Collins, Michael Foot and Jacquetta Hawkes and others were there to lead and to encourage. At the time we felt that our protest might well have some effect; in point of fact I doubt whether it achieved anything at all.

My marriage to Sylvia had not been a happy one since the end of the war; we just weren't right for each other, though we compromised while the children were young and gave no hint of the problems to people outside the family. I felt, after twenty-six years of marriage that I could not sustain the relationship any longer.

I met Eileen in 1962, when she was living in Canterbury and teaching English at Nonington, a PE college for women. Eileen is the most wonderful person I have ever met and we fell deeply in love, a love that has grown deeper and more wonderful over the 36 years we have been together. Without Eileen I should have succumbed to a life that was no more than an existence. She gave me the initiative to make the break that I had for so long dreamed of but had not had the courage to carry out on my own.

Eileen and I set up home together in October 1962. First, we rented a cottage at Sandgate, virtually on the beach. There was no garden as such, just a small square of concrete with a low wall to stop the waves from pounding the cottage windows. In practice, it didn't do this as the sea when rough pounded the shutters of the French windows and sent showers of shingle as high as the roof. But when the weather was fine and the sea calm, we could sit outside and watch the ships passing up and down the Channel. Gran came with us and enjoyed her declining years in a way that hadn't been possible since she left Ferring, ten years before. Eileen was still teaching at Nonington, but resigned soon afterwards as Sandgate would not have been suitable as a permanent home and we had ideas of moving to London. The winter of 1962-63 was severe; the snow was heavy and stayed around until April. It was very cold and the seagulls were starving. I used to get stale loaves from the baker and feed the birds on the wing. Hundreds of seagulls swarmed round the cottage and snapped up the bread as I tossed it into the air. However, Eileen and Gran and I were quite snug behind the shuttered windows.

We were looking for a flat in London and found a most attractive one to rent in Dulwich. We moved in April and our journey there was not without incident. I hired a van to take our belongings but on the journey our van suffered a burst tyre. We wanted to arrive before 5pm as I had a *Children's Hour* broadcast of *A Funny Thing Happened*, which we were hoping to listen to, but with a van of furniture to install and a burst tyre it didn't look hopeful. Eileen stayed with the van on the motorway and a kind motorist gave me a lift to the nearest town where I found a garage which provided a new tyre and transported me back to our accident spot. It's not every day that you can thumb a lift on a motorway and enjoy such a lucky set of circumstances, but this was 1962. Times have changed!

Eileen and I went to Oslo when the last Stompa film was being shot and had an interesting time on the set and in the surrounding countryside where the exterior shots were being filmed. When the last film (*Jennings of Course*) was having its premiere, we were invited over as guests for the first night.

Arriving in Oslo, we were told that the film was being shown at two different cinemas in the city on the same evening. We were taken to the first cinema where I was invited on to the stage and told to make a speech. I explained that my Norwegian was confined to two phrases so I spoke in English, which went down very well. I was presented with an enormous bouquet. As I staggered off-stage with my flowers they were immediately commandeered. I asked why and was told that we were now going over to the second cinema where a reception was awaiting us and the same bouquet would be presented to me at the end of the festivities. I was glad about this; two bouquets would have been more than I could have coped with.

Having taken over the Dulwich flat, the next thing to decide was the best plan to accommodate our mothers. Gran was now eighty and Eileen's mum was just a few years younger. She was still living in the house in Canterbury, which Eileen had bought when she was teaching at Nonington. We had no second bedroom in Dulwich, so we couldn't take Gran with us, so for a time we put the two mothers into the Canterbury house. It was only a temporary expedient but it worked very well until, later, we moved from Dulwich to Barcombe and settled the old ladies in a flat which we rented for them in Lewes. Eileen returned to her previous job at Dick Sheppard School and I went on writing my Jennings books and plays. There were a fair number of children's authors living around us and we decided to extend our membership of the Society of Authors, to which we belonged, to include a section for children's writers. Thus, the Children's Writers Group came into being and is still a useful limb of the Society.

In September 1963, Eileen was pregnant and Corin was on the way. This was just as we were enjoying our Norwegian visit to see the Stompa film. Eileen gave up her teaching job at the end of the

Christmas term. Corin was born at King's College Hospital, London in June 1964. The rented Wate's flat in Dulwich Wood Park was not a permanent solution to the housing problem and we decided we wanted to live in the country, but not too deeply into the sticks as I needed to get into London fairly frequently. Our friends Kathleen and Donald Mitchell, who lived in London, also rented a cottage at Barcombe Mills near Lewes and we had visited them several times during our sojourn in Dulwich. We found Barcombe an ideal place to live and bring up a young child and, when we heard that a cottage called East Crink would shortly be on the market, we got in touch with the owner who invited us to come down and see the property. We made up our minds on the spot; any delay would have meant that the cottage would at once be put on the market and our chance to buy it would be in some doubt. We made a wise decision; East Crink turned out to be an ideal home in a village where we have been happy to live ever since. Barcombe is a friendly place with a farming community interspersed with a number of people who had come to work at the new University of Sussex. There was also, when we first came, a fair number of British Raj who had come to spend their retirement in and around the village. We didn't have much in common with them politically, but this didn't seem to matter; we made some very good friends.

Corin thrived on the breezy air of Barcombe (and it can be very breezy with the wind in the south-west) and was made a great fuss of by the two grandmothers, who were sharing the flat we rented for them in Lewes. Sad to say, my mother died in June 1965 just before Corin's first birthday. Mum was nearly 82 when she had the final stroke. She was a woman loved by all who knew her; a kindly uncomplaining person who had been a widow ever since my father was killed in World War One; a marriage lasting seven years, followed by a widowhood of nearly fifty. Sally and Tim had grown up with Gran and were close to her in their childhood; sadly Corin can have no recollection of the grandmother who loved him very much. Eileen's mother, who was younger than Gran, died in 1973 so Corin, aged nine, has fond memories of her.

From an early age, Corin showed all the signs of being musical. He would sit silent and absorbed listening to the record player for long stretches at a time, and demand to hear his favourite tunes over and over again. His tastes were catholic and his demands included everything from Elizabeth Schwarzkopf to Gilbert & Sullivan and Flanders & Swann. Corin's musicality has ensured a privileged education for him. He entered New College School, Oxford as a chorister at the age of nine. From thence, he gained a music scholarship to Lancing and in 1973 he returned to Oxford as the Hadow Scholar at Worcester College. Since then he has made his living as a musician and is married to Laura, an actress.

I was still busy scribbling away in the sixties. I had had a TV series about Jennings on BBC some years before, but nothing further had come of it until quite by chance I had a stroke of luck. Frank Muir was in charge of BBC Light Entertainment at the time and rang up to ask me to write another series. It appeared that Frank knew nothing about my plays, but his son went to a prep school where my books were banned for the bizarre reason that the headmaster's name was Jennings and he thought that his dignity would be impaired by this hypothetical association. So, banned from reading Jennings at school, the boy was enjoying them at home. Frank cast an eye over his son's choice of book and immediately decided they would be good TV material. The moral of this anecdote is that for writers, actors, musicians – anybody trying to earn a living in the arts world – you need luck plus the ability to keep going.

A writer working in isolation is often in need of a change of literary scene and, in my case, this has taken the form of some sort of theatrical activity – either amateur or professional. In Lewes there is an excellent Little Theatre, which we joined shortly after we came to live in Barcombe. We took part in productions whenever we could, Eileen as a director, and later, Corin with his music. Three of my plays were produced here, two of them about Jennings, and a musical *It Happened In Hamelin* with musical score by Corin.

I was fortunate in being contracted to play small acting parts at Glyndebourne, which I did regularly for twelve years. I played in *Der Rosenkavalier, The Barber of Seville, Carmen, A Midsummer Night's Dream, Arabella, La Traviata* and several others. I also went on tour with the company for three years, playing from Manchester in the North to Plymouth and Southampton in the South.

I hardly need to add that as an actor I was permanently mute – indeed, I was not allowed to sing (though when on stage with the chorus I did, indeed, open my mouth and frame the words). It was a wonderful experience being directed by directors such as Peter Hall and John Cox; I had the best of both worlds, being involved with international class opera while knowing that as a non-singer I couldn't bring the performance crashing to a halt because I had forgotten my lines. Not that this state of affairs ever happened at Glyndebourne. The nearest we ever got to a calamity was when a famous German star was late for an entrance; the orchestra was silent and the cast on stage had to improvise until the culprit appeared, breathless from running from his dressing room.

I was also in the cast when *Albert Herring*, which we had done at Glyndebourne, was engaged for a season at the Royal Opera House in Covent Garden. Backstage at Covent Garden was a bewildering warren of corridors and staircases. I never could work out the geography of the place; I always managed to find my way to the stage in time, but I was never sure whether I should emerge in the wings at Stage Right or Stage Left. My last part at Glyndebourne was in *Don Giovanni*. This was the final production of the season, after which the Opera House was closed for a year for re-building.

9

There is a photograph on the bookshelf in our living room, which records the visit we paid to Bullecourt seventy-five years after my father was killed on that battlefield. My son, Tim, who lives in Barcombe with his partner, B, carried out the essential research because we had never been able to identify the exact place where my father met his death. Tim went to the headquarters of the Honourable Artillery Company in London and was able from their records to gain more detailed information than we had known about earlier. I regret that we had not done this before when my mother was alive, but, apart from Dad's letters, she had seemed rather reluctant to open old wounds by discussing the tragedy in much detail. It was after Mum died in 1965 that we came across more information amongst her possessions. With this information, Eileen compiled a book about Dad's poems and last letters from the time he was called up for the army. Tim's researches led to our little pilgrimage. Then, Corin, Eileen and I went first to Arras where we found Dad's name on the memorial to thousands of soldiers who had died on the battlefields in the region. We travelled on to Bullecourt and though the countryside was now very different we located as nearly as we could the remains of an old railway line which was mentioned in the records as the scene of the battle. Here we took the photo which now has pride of place on our bookshelf. In the village of Bullecourt, we met the mayor who opened for us the little museum commemorating the tragic days of May 1917. Three-quarters of a century later, artefacts are still being unearthed by the plough as the local farmers grow their crops in the fields, now returned to their natural use.

Our friend, Felicity Hayes-McCoy, who produces programmes for the BBC, is an admirer of my father's work. She compiled a programme for BBC Radio 4 about his poems and his death at Bullecourt. The programme was broadcast on my 85th birthday,

June 20th 1997. Some of dad's poems from his book *Spindrift* were read; Corin wrote the music and I talked about my life as a writer.

In retrospect, I have had a wonderfully fulfilled life with Eileen, my children and grandchildren, indeed all the members of my extended family have made my life memorably happy.

APPENDIX

THE JENNINGS ILLUSTRATORS

The first five Jennings books were not illustrated, but contained a dustjacket and frontispiece by Salomon van Abbe. Van Abbe then provided not only dustjacket and frontispiece but also line drawings for *According to Jennings*, the first Jennings title to be illustrated. Salomon van Abbe was born on 31st July 1883 in Amsterdam. He came to England when he was five, and studied in London at Kennington, Bolt Court, and the Central School of Arts and Crafts. He was well known as a painter and etcher of portraits. He did a good deal of travelling on the Continent, and often exhibited at the Royal Academy and the Royal Hibernian Academy. In 1933 he became a member of the Royal Society of British Artists, and during 1939 and 1940 he became president of the London Sketch Club. Examples of other books he illustrated, usually with line drawings, included the 1930 Duckworth edition of *Loyalties* by John Galsworthy, and the 1948 Dent edition of Louisa May Alcott's much-loved *Little Women*. He might well have gone on to illustrate more of the Jennings books but for his death in 1955, the year after *According to Jennings* was published.

The next thirteen Jennings titles were all illustrated, both pictures and dustjackets, by Douglas Mays. Mays also provided a new dustjacket illustration for a reprint of *Jennings Goes to School*, and colour frontispieces for the first six titles that he illustrated. Douglas Lionel Mays was born in August 1900, was educated at Kingston-upon-Thames and then studied at Goldsmiths' College School of Art. A painter in watercolour and oil, Mays used pen and pencil to illustrate children's school stories and adventure stories, and indeed he illustrated a large number of children's books, including works by Percy F.Westerman, Noel Streatfeild and Nancy Breary. He also exhibited at the Royal Academy and contributed drawings to several magazines, including *Punch*. It was as illustrator of the weekly articles in *Punch* which reported on world events that Mays was particularly successful. *The Jennings Report* was the last title for which Mays provided illustrations.

The next book, *Typically Jennings*, was not illustrated. The dustjacket and frontispiece were provided by Val Biro. Born in 1921 in Budapest, Biro illustrated vast numbers of books, mostly for children, and numerous other publications such as *Radio Times*. His most famous creation is Gumdrop, a vintage car based on his own 1926 Austin 12/4; Biro writes the stories and provides the illustrations for this series of books. He has recently agreed to illustrate Jennings once more by providing covers and line drawings for the publication of several volumes of the original radio playscripts under the titles *Jennings Sounds the Alarm, Jennings Breaks the Record, Jennings Joins the Search Party, Jennings to the Rescue,* and *Jennings and the Roman Remains*, with more to come.

The most famous illustrator to be associated with the Jennings books is Quentin Blake. He provided some pictures that were used in the 1970 adaptation of some of the Jennings stories for the BBC *Jackanory* programme. Blake is, of course, best known for his illustrations in the Roald Dahl books, and has also provided jacket illustrations for the Penguin editions of the works of Evelyn Waugh, Kingsley Amis and Malcolm Bradbury. Sadly for Jennings fans, none of Blake's artwork appeared in any of the Jennings books. In 1999 Blake became the first Children's Laureate.

The last two Jennings titles that were published by Collins, *Speaking of Jennings* and *Jennings at Large*, were not illustrated, nor was there a frontispiece illustration; the picture on the dustjacket of *Speaking of Jennings* was a photograph, and the cover illustration for *Jennings at Large*, which first appeared in paperback, was provided by Michael Brownlow. The very last two Jennings titles, published by Macmillan, were illustrated by Rodney Sutton. The line drawings were by Andrew (Andy) Lloyd-Jones. Born in 1963 in Denbigh, he studied at the Wrexham College of Art; moving to London in 1985, he provided illustrations for modern editions of the *William* and *Famous Five* stories as well as the two Jennings titles. He has now returned to North Wales.

Jennings on the Radio

It's just over 50 years since Anthony Buckeridge's *Jennings at School* took radio's Children's Hour by storm with Jennings' hilarious antics. His adventures were transferred to over twenty books that sold in their millions in the 50s and 60s. Sadly, the majority of the 62 radio recordings are lost, but here, published for the first time, are the first thirty-two of those plays for Jennings' countless fans to enjoy, each one delightfully and lovingly illustrated by Val Biro. All softback, A5 size, 160-176 pages, £12.00 each.

Volume 1 - Jennings Sounds the Alarm Why is Jennings standing in a puddle wearing only one shoe? Will Mr Wilkins get bitten by the Poisonous Spider and swell up like a barrage balloon? Do cats have two legs and a kitbag? Plays 1-7. ISBN 0 9521482 2 6

Volume 2 - Jennings Breaks the Record Will a broken back brake block break Jennings' journey? What will become of Darbishire's idea for a Society for the Prevention of Cruelty to Crocodiles on Sundays? Plays 8-14. ISBN 0 9521482 3 4

Volume 3 - Jennings Joins the Search Party Can Jennings and Darbishire plod homeward before the curfew tolls the knell of parting day, or will they be stuck in Pottlewhistle Halt for ever? Plays 15-20. ISBN 0 9521482 4 2

Volume 4 - Jennings to the Rescue Discover the true identity of Jennings' mysterious friends Selbanev, Nosnikta and Snikliw. Do they really belong to the Moscow Dynamos football team, or is Jennings embroiled with subversive Russian agents? Plays 21-26. ISBN 0 9521482 5 0

Volume 5 - Jennings and the Roman Remains Why is a disused wheel once belonging to a Linbury Corporation dust-cart being exhibited between a fragment of fourth century hypocaust and the spear of a Roman Centurion? Plays 27-32. ISBN 0 9521482 6 9

DS

David Schutte : 119 Sussex Road : Petersfield : Hampshire : GU31 4LB